THE "NEW MONARCHIES"
AND REPRESENTATIVE ASSEMBLIES

Medieval Constitutionalism or Modern Absolutism?

PROBLEMS IN EUROPEAN CIVILIZATION

UNDER THE EDITORIAL DIRECTION OF

Ralph W. Greenlaw* and Dwight E. Lee†

Other volumes in preparation

PROBLEMS IN EUROPEAN CIVILIZATION

THE "NEW MONARCHIES" AND REPRESENTATIVE ASSEMBLIES

Medieval Constitutionalism or Modern Absolutism?

EDITED WITH AN INTRODUCTION BY

Arthur J. Slavin, BUCKNELL UNIVERSITY

D. C. HEATH AND COMPANY · BOSTON

Table of Contents

Introduction

THE problem of the "New Monarchy" is a genuine one. The inquiring student needs look no farther afield than the first two volumes of the *New Cambridge Modern History* to ascertain that fact. He might reasonably expect the work in question to provide a relatively consistent view of monarchy as it existed in Europe north of the Alps, between the Elbe and the Pyrenees, in the late fifteenth and sixteenth centuries. Quite the contrary! Professor Denys Hay, in his "Introduction" to the first volume, notes a prevailing tendency to absolute monarchy distinguishing the period 1493–1520.[1] Whereas Dr. G. R. Elton, summarizing the contents of the second volume, while admitting the growing strength of the secular state, warns against the easy acceptance of the "New Monarchy" thesis. "In truth," he notes, "these western monarchies were less autocratic and self-consciously innovatory than is commonly supposed. By comparison with the despots of the East . . . they were as yet a long way from the absolutism of the seventeenth century. Everywhere there survived remnants of past separatism and constitutional rights. . . ."[2]

Lest it be argued that English scholars are simply more querulous than their continental counterparts, we may note the same sort of disagreement among leading French and German historians. Roland Mousnier, one of France's most distinguished historians, holds that about 1500 "The majority of states were evolving towards absolute monarchy."[3] His promi-

nent colleague, the late Henri Hauser, expressed the same view in his masterful study of the sixteenth century: "Everywhere, one may say, the hereditary monarchies evolved towards absolutism."[4] Their countryman Leon Cahen, on the other hand, ventured emphatic disagreement. Speaking specifically of England, he noted the widespread lack of consensus about what the words "New Monarchy" denoted. He was driven to conclude that "if there was a new monarchy under Henry VII it was in this sense: that he reestablished the strong kingship of the past centuries. The Tudor monarchy was the resurrection of a tradition."[5] Gerhardt Ritter, perhaps the greatest of present-day German historians, agrees with Mousnier and Hartung. In his chief work on the sixteenth century he speaks of beginning "the history of the new, the absolute monarchies," with the generation of kings that includes Henry VII of England and Louis XI of France.[6]

In pointing out the real disagreement about the meaning of the term "New Monarchy" as applied generally to the regimes of the late fifteenth and early sixteenth centuries, and the further implication that the monarchies in question were "new" in the sense of belonging to the modern rather than the medieval period of European history, one has only opened the inquiry. What exactly was the nature of these monarchies? That question cannot be simply answered by reference to an-

[1] *New Cambridge Modern History*, I, 8.
[2] *New Cambridge Modern History*, II, 8.
[3] *Les XVIᵉ et XVIIᵉ Siècles* (Paris, 1956), p. 109.
[4] *Les Debuts de L'Age Moderne* (Paris, 1956), p. 7.
[5] *L'Évolution Politique de L'Angleterre* (Paris, 1960), p. 16.
[6] *Die Neugestaltung Europas in 16. Jahrhundert* (Berlin, 1950), p. 30.

other term, be it absolutism or any syno-
nym chosen for the purpose of labelling
the complex of institutions comprehended
by the "New Monarchy" label itself. The
historian and the student of history alike
must always be wary of mere definitions.
It is their obligation to seek to know something more substantial about the meaning
of the term, especially as it may be expressed in details drawn from the history
of particular countries and the reigns of
particular kings.

As one begins to examine the facts behind the label, old familiar data come to
mind in a richness of detail. One recalls
the oft-repeated accounts describing the
England of Henry VII after the victory
over the Yorkists at Market Bosworth, or
the France of Charles VIII and Louis XI,
slowly recovering from the ravage of the
Hundred Years' War. For more than a century aristocratically inspired anarchy, royal
incapacity and waning clerical dominance
had beset a society once seemingly articu-
lated in three orders of warriors, workers
and worshipful priests. The Black Death
crept in with rats and lice, contributing to
the untuning of the string of order, while
peasants jostled the noblesse as arable gave
way to pasture in a countryside Thomas
More complained of when he noted that
sheep threatened to eat up men! A European *Zeitenwende* or time of troubles was
at hand. The fabric of the old Europe was
rent. Such is the picture constituting the
stock in trade of historians of the early
modern period.

The historians perhaps unconsciously
emulated the thought of the men of the
waning middle ages they wrote about in
their abhorrence of a vacuum—even a
chronological one! Something had to fill
the void left by the collapse of the old order vividly proclaimed by both chroniclers
and poets. Because collapse was not followed by dissolution something new must
have come to fill the void. The "New
Monarchy" was the answer!

A new Europe was called into being, as
if by a second act of creation. Historians

eagerly described new dynasties or those
re-invigorated royal lines which were just
as good as new ones. A halo of novelty
surrounded every aspect of the age. The
Roman church and the decadent feudatories were eclipsed along with the other
forces of medieval particularism and provincialism. A new style of absolute centralized government grew up, with new
techniques of justice, new administrative
organs, new assertions of the royal prerogative and new uses for proud assemblies
of the realm that had first appeared in the
forgotten middle ages. The "New Monarchies," it was argued, were centralized
states in the modern fashion, over which
kings presided *de leur puysance absolue*
—by virtue of their absolute power—without regard to the restraints inherent in the
old ideals which had placed limits upon
secular power. These limits which were
best typified by feudal ideas of contract,
the vast structure of the Catholic Church
and the maxims of Roman law which
taught that "what concerned all had to
have the consent of all," were now set
aside. The modern state was trumpeted
onto the stage of history, absolute in character and impatient of the multiplicity of
authorities that characterized the medieval
world-view. The new Messiah was the
king.

In place of the old unity in multiplicity
historians found a simple new unity best
represented by that terrible maxim of the
Roman law: *quod principem placuit habet
legis vigorem* (whatever pleases the prince
has the force of law). Historians wrote a
new primer, complete with a new Three
R's: The Renaissance; the Reformation;
and the Reception of Roman law. The
first provided the secular and individualist
impulse capitalized upon by the kings.
The second ended forever the absurdity of
divided sovereignty, bringing to a close the
era of papal tutelage. The third pushed
into the farthest recesses of thought the
notion of consent. That was the classic
pattern presented by A. F. Pollard's *Factors in Modern History* in 1907. He be-

lieved the dialectic of history had moved relentlessly beyond its medieval phase. Hair-splitters might quibble about the event which started the modern world on its way, with some opting for Charles VIII's victory over his Estates-General in 1484, while others accepted the more martial triumph of Henry Tudor at Bosworth in the following year. What matter? The "New Monarchies" had come into being; their rise was accompanied by the sensible decline of representative institutions.

The modern state seen by Pollard had both negative and positive supporting struts. On the positive side were to be found nationalism, the rise of bureaucratic administration, the emergence of the middle class firmly allied with ruling dynasties and the developing idea of absolutism. Negatively considered, the emergent states rested on the decline of the aristocracy, the ruin of the church and the decadence of parliamentarism. Pollard's view has been vigorously championed in more recent times by Roland Mousnier, who incorporated into his restatement of the thesis a wealth of detail utilizing data developed in more recent social and economic studies of the period. Mousnier, however, to a greater degree than Pollard, recognizes the survival of limiting agencies from the medieval epoch and recognizes also that fully developed absolutism emerged only after a period of evolutionary development. Both the essence of Pollard's original statement and Mousnier's affirmative revision are here presented under the rubric of The "New Monarchy" Thesis.

Almost every aspect of his thesis has received careful scrutiny in the generation since Pollard's *Factors* was first published. It would take several volumes like the present one to discuss the work of scholars who either support or disavow the thesis in every particular. The role of the aristocracy, the gentry, the merchant-princes, the churchmen and the bureaucrats has been carefully evaluated. The nature of central government and its relation to the declining feudatories has provoked talk of "aris-

tocratic resurgence" and "renascent fiscal feudalism." The structural supports of the thesis, both positive and negative, have been tested, with the result that some are now accepted and others found wanting.

Because the literature is so voluminous and the problem so complex, it is clearly impossible to try to deal with it in its totality. For this reason, the essays in this volume will focus solely on the related themes of the expansion of princely government, the centralization of power, and the interaction of these with the traditions of representative institutions.

Pollard's consideration of the relationship of princes and parliaments clearly implies, and on this point he has the support of Mousnier, that there was a contest for power in the early modern period in which absolutist sovereigns triumphed over long-standing but often decadent traditions of consent. It also brings us to grips with the problem of the proper periodic designation for the monarchies in question, and some historians have been much agitated by Pollard's attempt to impose a fairly sharp medieval-modern dialectic as implicit in the work of Henry VII, Francis I, Gustavus Vasa and their contemporaries.

The next light essays, therefore, deal with the two related themes of the assertion of royal authority in government and the role played by representative assemblies especially with respect to the question of whether they limited or extended royal powers. Essays focusing on England, France, Burgundy and the Netherlands, Sweden and the Germanies provide a sufficient range of data drawn from the period of the late fifteenth and sixteenth centuries to insure that the meaning and applicability of Pollard's thesis on a European scale can be evaluated.

In the first of these, Professor Walter C. Richardson selects finance as the key to measuring the effectiveness of government under the early Tudors. On the basis of much careful archival research, he presents arguments both for and against the traditional view of the modernity of Tudor government. While, on the one hand, he approves of the term "New Monarchy" to describe Henry VII's regime, and readily agrees with Pollard that centralization of authority seemed to go forward at the expense of some older traditionally limiting interests, yet he also insists that Henrician government rested on medieval household organs reminiscent of those described in the justly famous studies by Thomas Frederick Tout of medieval governmental administration.[7] Similarly Professor Richardson paradoxically emphasizes the *practical* absolutism of Henry VII and Henry VIII in summing up Tudor practice, while at the same time stressing their ability to make the best of the growing power of parliament, in contrast to the Stuarts who held to a rigid doctrine of *theoretical* absolutism and at the same time were unable to solve the problem of how to deal with the unruly body which occasionally had to be convened at Westminster.

Richardson's emphasis on continuity in governmental technique under the early Tudors was sharply challenged by Dr. G. R. Elton of Cambridge University. Their overall interpretations of what the Tudors had done in the way of changing the monarchy in England could hardly have been more divergent. Dr. Elton insists that medieval government was fundamentally government emanating from the king's person and his immediate entourage, while early modern government was basically independent of the royal household and was bureaucratically organized in national departments responsible to a crown whose ultimate power was rooted in parliamentary enactments. By his own criteria Elton was forced to concede that Cardinal Wolsey, for all his autocratic manner, merely restored good medieval government, whereas, only a few years later, no matter how hard a successor in office, Thomas Cromwell, labored to disguise his work under the

forms of doing business inherited from the past, his actions constituted a "revolution" in government. That revolution in government saw royal power claiming support of a truly national sovereignty established on the basis of parliamentary statutes, the effect of which was to create the modern, monarchic, nation-state. Thus Elton seemingly accepts one of Pollard's main contentions, merely delaying the appearance of the "New Monarchy" by a half century, while representing the radical refashioning of government as, in large measure, a product of the Reformation. We find to our surprise that neither Professor Richardson nor Dr. Elton rejects Pollard's usage entirely, although for the former it was more medieval than modern; for the latter it was not the result of royal initiative at all. Both agree in insisting on the vitality of parliament: Richardson seeing it chiefly as a useful annoyance to the Tudors which became a mere annoyance to the Stuarts, while for Elton its role was more positive, since it was the foundation stone of the modern state. But both make careful qualifications of the term absolutism, modifying it enough to make us wonder to what extent it is meaningful to describe the Tudor monarchy as either new or absolute?

The theme of centralization as one of the primary aims of the "New Monarchs" caught the attention of the great Belgian historian Henri Pirenne. In an important article on the Burgundian state he exposed the difficulties of a sovereign ruler in a state lacking in both ethnic and linguistic homogeneity. At the same time he tried to demonstrate that the Burgundian state was consciously built on the "modern" idea of unification, even though he was well aware of the medieval diversity which survived as the basic substratum of the monarch's power. He makes it clear that the Burgundian dukes and the Hapsburgs had to try to fashion a centralized state primarily by building upon the person powers concentrated in their hands as great feudal suzerains in much the same way as the Capetians and other feudal monarchs had

[7] The reference is to the ground-breaking six volumes that appeared under the general title *Chapters in the Administrative History of Medieval England* (Manchester, 1920–1933).

fashioned their states in an earlier period. Read in this way, the history of the constitution in the Burgundian Netherlands seemed to follow the typical pattern of state-building used by nationally-minded princes seeking unity on the basis of dynastic principles, hardly a modern feature, and the old feudal ideals of local authorities hierarchically arranged. In describing the Burgundian dukes' efforts to centralize, Pirenne noted without offering detailed evidence that the Burgundian rulers consciously tried to use assemblies of representatives of the provinces formed in States General as a tool in unification. Traditions of local particularism, however, in the provincial assemblies proved to be too strong to make even the States General an effective force for unity. In this affirmation Pirenne departs radically from the traditional view of royal policy in the age of the "New Monarchy," a view in which rulers were held to be the destroyers of representative assemblies that loomed as rivals in the struggle for power.

A contemporary scholar, H. G. Koenigsberger, coming back in part to the same ground a half century later, sees the problem of the relationship between the monarchy and the States General in the Netherlands more in terms of the traditional "New Monarchy" thesis. He rejects Pirenne's view that the Burgundian dukes consciously tried to use the unifying potential of the States General to augment their recognized authority as feudal suzerains. In fact, he suggests that while their policy towards it seems at times to have been ambivalent, they recognized that the States General had played a really revolutionary role in the 1470's and 1480's, usurping certain monarchical functions, and therefore they never ceased to regard it more as a dangerous rival than as a potentially useful ally. But even had the rulers accepted this latter view, Koenigsberger stresses that the States General could only have been of limited usefulness because it was energized by a self-destructive principle. It was never anything more than a "congress of

delegates from quasi-autonomous powers" and, as such, able to put up a stubborn passive resistance against any national policies proposed by the prince but unable to institute or carry out any national policies of their own except in consequence of some rare emergency facing the people. Medieval particularism of the kind found in the Netherlands cannot be classed as "constitutionalism" opposed to growing "absolutism." It represented the triumph of local privileges and autonomy as voiced by prelates, nobles and the patrician oligarchies of the towns. Against that array of forces, whatever centralizing policies were attempted ended in failure. This close study of the States General might be said to show that the "New Monarchy" attempted by the Burgundian dukes and Hapsburg regents failed because they, unlike their successful fellow rulers, were unable to overcome the forces of particularism. The States General of the Netherlands never did duplicate the sense of England's parliament, in which the "community of the realm" found its voice. One more thing is worthy of noting here. Contrary to the "New Monarchy" thesis, the failure of Renaissance monarchy in the Netherlands seems to show the vitality of medieval particularism, despite the urbanization and "modernization" of the economic life of that part of Europe, just as a similar degree of vitality was shown by the equally advanced and equally independent Italian and German cities. Far from the *bourgeoisie* rallying to the support of the "New Monarchy," the urban patriciate led the assemblies in resisting royal policy. The monarchy failed precisely because there was no united *nation* to support the *state*, a fact that attempted borrowings by the rulers, first from French and then from Imperial constitutional models, could not overcome. Pirenne and Koenigsberger thus agree on this much: monarchy in the Burgundian Netherlands was never successful and never absolute. Both adduce some evidence which challenges Pollard's views; both equally contribute some evidence supporting them, while undermining the utility of the medieval-modern dialectic when it is applied to the Netherlands. The reality proved too complex!

Turning to France in this period, the problem seems to be less complicated as the lines of the nation and the state appear to be so clearly etched. The French monarchy in the early modern era has been the major concern of J. Russell Major. His several books and articles based on detailed archival research have suggested some interesting revisions of previously accepted conclusions. Professor Major agrees in part with the classic thesis: the sixteenth century followed hard on the heels of an earlier royal drive to consolidate central authority in the aftermath of the disasters suffered in the wars against England and the domestic strife of the fifteenth century. But, he asks, was that drive not frustrated by a number of factors? In addition to the continued supremacy of the nobility, the traditions of corporatism expressed by lawyers in the provincial *parlements* and the inability of the crown to raise an effective standing army, he adds the financial crisis of the age as a force compelling the Renaissance kings in France, especially Francis I and Henry II, to solicit the support of the traditional representative institutions. He suggests that the cessation of activity by the Estates General between 1484 and 1560 seems to have misled older historians and caused them to look upon the era as one of royal absolutism. He corrects this view by pointing out that the *parlements* and the provincial estates played a most effective role in limiting the supposed absolutism of Francis I. He goes on to show that despite the grandeur of his court and the pretension of the royal style, Francis I literally thought of himself as the first gentleman of the realm! The historian who pays close attention to sixteenth century monarchy in France must conclude that it was in most essentials just a continuation of the monarchy of Charles VII, and as such was to endure until at least the reign of Louis XIII. Far from seeing France as

a model of continental absolutism in the fashion popularized during the era of the Renaissance by English critics like Sir John Fortescue, who spoke of France as a "Turkish despotism," Major disagrees with Mousnier and proclaims the sixteenth century French monarchy to be a "consultative monarchy" which changed into an efficiently run, centralized state only a century later, during the Thirty Years' War, under the guidance of Richelieu, whose spiritual heir Colbert completed the process of building a rational, absolute and modern state in France.

We have seen that historians whose special interest lies in England, Burgundy and France have formulated serious reservations about the applicability of the Pollard-Mousnier analysis. They have either the modernity of the monarchies in question or their absolutism; sometimes they have done both. The continued importance of particularist forces and traditional constitutional forms, often eloquently embodied in the colloquies of parliamentary assemblies, is a striking commentary on the character of European politics in an age of apparently growing monarchical power. With this in mind, if we turn to the north, especially to Sweden, and look to the east of the Rhine, to the Germanies, even more arresting signs of the vitality of representative institutions present themselves.

F. L. Carsten in his book on the politics of the German states from the fifteenth to the eighteenth centuries focuses on the power struggle waged by princes and parliaments for generations after the collapse of Imperial authority signalled by the issuance of the Golden Bull of 1356, a document which merely made official what had been a fact for some time. The Empire had failed to establish genuine sovereignty at the expense of the princes. In the wake of the death struggle with the papacy, and aided in part by the Interregnum of 1250–1272, both the princes and the ministerial nobility conspired to render the central power of the emperors a figment. The fourteenth and early fifteenth century witnessed political collapse in the territorial states as well, as various leagues, robber barons and dynastic wars engulfed the German states, petty and great alike. As the fifteenth century progressed, however, a revival of princely interest and competence took place, with Roman law maxims emphasizing sovereign powers eagerly seized on by the princes seeking to combat the many centrifugal forces, especially those represented in the various estates. The battlefields were smaller than those of England or France, but the struggles were of a similar nature. In order to solve the religious and economic problems of the late fifteenth and early sixteenth centuries, the German princes found it necessary to "work on" the particularist sympathies of the various elements in the Estates until a common sense of interest in the well-being of the territorial state was formed. Despite the alleged incapacity of the modern German when faced with the burden of political liberty, the records investigated by Carsten suggest that in an earlier period a capacity to deal with the problem was not lacking. Not only in lawmaking, but in practical administration as well, the German rulers relied on their parliaments in a manner not much different than that so familiar in medieval England.

The very essentials of the turn toward modernity in Germany were found in techniques borrowed from the Estates by the princes. Thus many German states tended to evolve along institutional lines very much like those found elsewhere in western Europe. When looked at in this way the institutional development of Germany in the sixteenth century is simply a part of a larger movement. The "New Monarchies" in Germany — and Carsten accepts that concept as applicable to his own area of interest — were real enough, although they were far from absolute in the sixteenth century. The essence of the monarchical regime was simply the reduction of the forces of anarchy, an achievement impossible without the aid of the constitutional principle represented by the Estates which had earlier appeared as just another divisive element in Imperial politics. Only after parliamentary assemblies gave proof that they could not maintain their position in the face of the crises of destructive warfare in the seventeenth century was absolutism possible in the Germanies. The resolution of medieval tensions in politics came only at the end of the confessional wars, when absolute monarchies, which by then were not *new,* overcame the dying constitutionalism of the representative assemblies.

In German principalities as in England and France, as well as in the Burgundian Netherlands, the sixteenth century appears as one of transition, a period in which medieval and modern concepts and forms of government jostle one another restlessly. "New monarchies" are indeed taking shape. But not apparently in the sense maintained by Pollard. If we turn to Sweden, which in the early sixteenth century was itself emerging from a catastrophic time of troubles, the already familiar contours of the problem achieve ever sharper definition.

The modern Swedish monarchy presides over one of the most advanced social democracies in the world. In few places can such an effective marriage of royal and parliamentary principles of government be found. Between our own day and the reforms of Gustavus Adolphus in the early seventeenth century, vigorous changes which capped the modern development took place. But even before that time there were currents of constitutionalism, of ideals and practices anticipatory of parliamentary monarchy. The historian of evolutionary beliefs would suspect that, even if he did not have the proof available.

Ingvar Andersson's *History of Sweden,* the work of a noted sixteenth century scholar and archivist, supplies the needed proof, while at the same time affording us further insights into the meaning of Pollard's terminology. As Dr. Andersson himself writes, in the age of the sixteenth century king, Gustavus Vasa, "the ideas of the medieval world were in the melting pot." The discovery of America, Magellan's circumnavigation of the world, the theological discoveries of Martin Luther — these were developments that coincided with the efforts of Vasa to forge a unified national state in place of the great dream of a Nordic kingdom embracing Denmark and Norway as well as Sweden itself. Building on the work of Karl Knutsson and the Stures, Vasa, as Gustav Eriksson of Rydboholm came to be known, founded a "New Monarchy." But the road was not an easy one. Opposition came from some of the old nobility, loathe to surrender feudal prerogatives, as well as from the peasants, conservative by nature and uneasy about church reform. In order to gain wider acceptance for the many innovations planned in church and state, especially acquiescence in administrative reforms and the disposition of church property in the course of the Reformation, Vasa found it necessary to turn to the Swedish Estates, the *Riksdag* or assembly already possessed of a long-standing history of participation in government. Sweeping aside the resistance of churchmen, provincial governors and the influence of the independent cities of the Hanseatic League, Vasa had by the early 1530's, with the aid of the *Riksdag*, established in Sweden a state quite like the one molded by Thomas Cromwell in England. It was a "New Monarchy" with a strong, centralized government.

In some respects Andersson found the break with the past to be complete. Yet in his narrative one cannot for very long escape the omnipresent *Riksdag*, itself a part of the medieval heritage and a bulwark of constitutional limits set to the authority of the newly crowned king. Between the Stures dream of a strong nation-state, which Vasa was able to realize, and the idea of absolutism, which Vasa neither sought nor realized, there stood the representative institutions of the Swedes, another instance of the subtle way in which

the old and the new combined in the sixteenth century to make it neither medieval nor modern.

It is hard to avoid over-stating the importance of parliamentary bodies in the European political system of the late fifteenth and early sixteenth centuries in a work focusing on the applicability of Pollard's thesis in the light of recent research and synthesis. Surely the role of such groups in the Netherlands and in England was strikingly different than it was in France, where the central Estates General suffered an early eclipse. Yet in France representative assemblies other than the Estates General continued to be important in the supposedly model despotism of the age. These and other points were ably made by Robert H. Lord in 1930, in a paper read at the annual meeting of the American Catholic Historical Association under the title, "The Parliaments of the Middle Ages and the Early Modern Period." That work is presented as the final essay in part two of this book, chiefly because it argues effectively for a line of criticism subsequently developed by more recent critics of the Pollard-Mousnier thesis. Lord shows that the hallmark of sixteenth century monarchy consisted more often than not in power *shared* between the representatives of the politically active classes and the royal administration. To that sharing, Lord gave the name "quasi-constitutionalism." What such a wording lacks in felicity is amply compensated for by its very suggestiveness of the limitations faced by the "New Monarchies."

This sampling of the results of recent scholarship has by choice focused on a single aspect of the problem of the sixteenth century monarchies and their immediate fifteenth century roots. Equal concentration on other facets would doubtlessly uncover further ambiguities and difficulties inherent in Pollard's formula when applied on a European scale. Yet the primary query remains unanswered unless we can characterize these facts still studied by historians under old rubrics.

No easy answer springs to mind. Professors Mousnier and Hartung had all they could do in 1955 merely to catalogue the problems implicit in any consideration of absolutism, when they addressed an international congress of historians at Rome.[8] This is not intended as a counsel of despair, however. Fortunately we can turn to the reconstructions attempted by J. Russell Major and J. H. Hexter, which, when taken together, seem to point a way for the next generation to follow.

It is perhaps not unfair to say that Major still values the term "New Monarchy" highly, though in a special sense: he wishes to preserve the view that the Renaissance, with which he associates the monarchies at issue, was an age of profound innovation. Hexter, on the other hand, is tired of orthodoxies and wants to start afresh, with a new vocabulary that tends to be as dialectical as that used by Pollard. His theses and antitheses are more subtle, surely, and they help us to find our way through a mass of data whose production increases at a nonlinear rate. Major and Hexter highlight a paradox implicit in the problem we are studying, a paradox that must be dealt with before bringing this essay to its close.

We live in an age beset with revolutionary tensions. Pollard lived and found his framework for historical thought in the late Victorian era, characteristically optimistic about the course of *evolution*. Yet he spoke of the revolutionary newness of the Renaissance monarchies. And it is just this point that seems to divide the syntheses of Hexter and Major. The former accuses Pollard of imposing a too evolutionary scheme of the data. Major, for his part, criticizes the details of Pollard's picture, but wishes to retain the essence of the Renaissance as marking a new era in human history, much in the fashion of Jacob Burckhardt. While each of our revisionists

insists that a new detailed vocabulary is needed, if we are ever to come to grips with the complex institutional changes of the period, there is between them an explicit disagreement about the lines of reconstruction. Both seem to reject the accidental features Pollard described as necessary parts of the "New Monarchy"; but each accepts the central notion of the essential newness of the period ca. 1450–1600. The business of working toward an adequate historical language with which to describe the balance of continuity and change thus looms as one of the great methodological challenges facing the next generation of historians.

The old formulas have come to play the part of a worn-out myth, a myth that once evoked thought and challenged the imagination but eventually grew stale and served to stifle further creative effort. Nobody will question that profound changes were taking place in the political institutions of Europe during the period under consideration here. Many will not question the utility of the term "New Monarchy" itself. But the myth represented by the neat dialectic expressed in the dichotomy "medieval-modern" makes neither Major nor Hexter happy. The medieval-modern antithesis almost always suggests another that might be referred to as the "constitutionalism-absolutism" framework. Such pairs of terms run the risk of bringing the historian to rest on the precariously sharp point of his own dialectical knife.

That is not to say that the revisionists have not their positive side. The "New Monarchy," with all of its implications, does not seem a wholly perverse idea to them, if by that formula we indicate the efforts made by princes and kings to cope with the besetting problems of government that each state faced during the late fifteenth and early sixteenth centuries, although not always at the same moment in time. If we can abandon the habit of looking at the concept as marking the end of the medieval era, which view Pollard and his supporters seemed to expound, and be-

[8] "Quelques problèmes concernant la monarchie absolue," *Relazioni del X congresso internazionale di scienze storiche* (Florence, 1955), IV, 1–55 (*Storia moderna*).

gin to treat the complex of ideas implied in the formula as nothing more than a descriptive framework within rough periodic limitations, then the "New Monarchy" ought to continue to stimulate the historians of future generations. In that way the historian, whose work is on the surface *conservative* of the past, can pour new wine into a valuable and favored old bottle, while avoiding the uncomfortable sensations arising when one rests on a point valuable in logic but of dubious worth in the looking-glass of historical fact.

[NOTE: all selections reprinted here omit the notes appearing in the original writings unless otherwise stated. All other notes are those supplied by the editor.]

"The circumstances of which we have been speaking in connection with the New Monarchy were anything but favourable to the development of Parliamentary independence and prestige. Indeed, everywhere but in England Parliamentary institutions almost disappeared."

— ALFRED FREDERICK POLLARD

"The progress of the absolute monarchies was not caused solely by the desire of the kings to increase their power. . . . The theory of absolutism answered the dominant needs of the societies and a desire of the *corps social*. Finally, the new monarchies were a result of the rivalries of two classes, the nobility and the bourgeoisie. The king had need of the latter in financial affairs. . . ."

— ROLAND MOUSNIER

"The newness of the Tudor rule lay . . . in the thoroughness with which it was administered. Old institutions were invigorated and adapted to new uses, while newer agencies followed the traditional pattern. . . . New policies were formulated, but ancient laws and traditional practices were observed. . . ."

— WALTER CECIL RICHARDSON

"Talk of a 'new monarchy' in the sixteenth century has become a little unfashionable of late. . . . But in some ways the reaction has gone too far; as regards political and social structure, the sixteenth century produced something quite new in England. . . ."

— GEOFFREY RUDOLPH ELTON

"As it appeared at the time of Philip the Good . . . the Burgundian State may be defined as a plurality of autonomous territories forming a monarchical unity. A certain equilibrium was established . . . between the local liberties and the princely power. Had it been free to develop itself at will, the latter would have arrived at absolutism. . . ."

— HENRI PIRENNE

". . . The States General of the Netherlands maintained itself only in the seven northern provinces of the Burgundian dominions; but there its victory was so decisive that, at least formally, it displaced the monarchy altogether."

— HELMUT GEORG KOENIGSBERGER

". . . the popular, consultative nature of the monarchy continued unmodified for the first third of the period and was only mildly altered thereafter. . . . Francis I had 'neither the strength of mind nor the steadfastness of will to apply himself to a systematic transformation of society and institutions.' "

— J. RUSSELL MAJOR

"In other words, the tendency to denigrate the German Estates and side with the princes, who tried to suppress them, persists to the present day. . . ."

— FREDERIC L. CARSTEN

"In the royal proclamations which were read before the Estates, Gustavus Vasa affirmed that *he* had fulfilled all his obligations to the people, but that the *people* had not responded in kind. . . . The fault was . . . that his project for a centralized administration under his direct control was incompatible with the medieval system. . . ."

— CARL INGVAR ANDERSSON

"It is largely, though perhaps not sufficiently, recognized that in the general scheme of the evolution of European states, between the age of feudalism and the era of absolute monarchy, there intervenes a period of what may be called parliamentary monarchy. . . ."

— ROBERT HOWARD LORD

". . . the Renaissance Monarchs put theory into practice by endeavoring to use representative institutions as a means of winning popular support for their program. . . ."

— J. RUSSELL MAJOR

"Thus, the chapter on 'The New Monarchy' demonstrates the triumphant political embodiment of the principle of nationality in the persons of the monarchs of the sixteenth century. . . . Thus . . . medieval history ended and modern history began."

— J. H. HEXTER

THE "NEW MONARCHY" THESIS: TOWARDS ABSOLUTISM

ALFRED F. POLLARD

A. F. Pollard was born in 1869. After a distinguished undergraduate career at Jesus College, Oxford, he took an M.A. in history. He wrote a number of distinguished books about Tudor history, was the recipient of numerous academic honors and prizes, among them the Lothian Prize and the Arnold Prize, and was made a Fellow of both the Royal Historical Society and of the British Academy. In addition he was an academic statesman of unrivaled vision, whose chief contribution to learning was not in his many volumes but in the Institute of Historical Research, London, which he founded.

I n my first lecture I drew your attention to the fact that, whereas ancient history deals mainly with the City-state and medieval history with the World-state, modern history is concerned principally with the national State; and to-day my object is to illustrate the development of the national State, particularly as represented by what we call the New Monarchy. For that is one of the prime factors in the history of the sixteenth century. The abstract idea of the State has been expressed in various forms; it has been cast in one mould after another, and so far it has found its most complete and effective expression in the national State. . . .

For the state in its infancy may be likened unto a little child. It has no ideas of its own and its earliest utterances are merely the repetition of what it has heard. . . . Now the child is generally given a governess; so is the State, and its governess is the Church. And the first thing the governess says is "you must be good. . . ." This is the function of the Church in the Dark and Middle Ages, to educate these growing states in the proper notions of right and wrong, to uphold a standard higher than that of force and fraud, and to set the moral above and before the material order of things. . . .

As time went on, however, the State began to develop ideas of its own; legislation begins to be something more than the statement of ancient custom. It begins to enunciate new principles, and the State to enforce them. The State in fact has developed a will of its own, and then the differences with the governess begin. . . . The result of this battle royal is still disputed: whether the victory really lay with the State or the Church, the child was not yet old enough to do without the governess; and it remained in somewhat sulky tutelage, with occasional rebellions, until the sixteenth century. Its sovereignty was denied, and it spent its time, not so much in governing, as in struggling for existence. But by the sixteenth century the child had grown to lusty youth, if not to manhood. The governess was dismissed with what she thought a very inadequate pension; and we hear much of the great spoliation made by Henry VIII. The State now boldly claimed omnipotence; and the claim is most forcibly and logically expressed in the *Leviathan* of Thomas Hobbes — the best philosophical comment extant on the Tudor system, al-

From A. F. Pollard, *Factors in Modern History* (London, 1907), pp. 52–73, 93. Reprinted by permission of Constable and Company Limited, and The Beacon Press.

though it was written in Stuart times. Sovereignty, he explained, must be absolute, though the sovereign need not be a monarch. . . . It may be unwise or unjust for the State to do various things; but if it does those things by proper constitutional methods, their legal authority cannot be denied, though their moral validity may be impugned. Within the limits of human possibility, the State has become omnipotent; its growth is complete; from a creation it has become a creator.

This complex and abstract conception of the State has only been evolved by a slow and painful process. The Teutonic invaders of Great Britain had scarcely any notion of the State; their state was simply their kindred, their blood relations. They knew of no such thing as treason; all crimes were merely offences against the kindred, and might be redeemed by money payments to the family. This family system broke down under the stress of war and migration, which produced a specialised military class; and the chief of this class became the king. The Church baptized what war had begotten; and the king became gradually the anointed of God, the fountain of honour and justice, and lord first of the people, and then of their land. He symbolised the unity of his people, and his authority grew in degree as it expanded in area. . . . The king is for long the only national representative, and round him centre such national aspirations as emerge from the conflict of local passions. National unity is only personal; the king is the State; treason is an offence against him; and it required a very arbitrary straining of the law to bring it to bear against Strafford with the idea that treason was really an offence against the State, of which the king was only an ornamental expression.

Feudalism, however, was an uncongenial soil for absolute monarchy. The king was the theoretical apex of civilisation, the head of everything; but practice robbed him of most of his powers, and divided them among his barons. The king was *primus inter pares,* little more; and all the talk

about divine right, absolute power, and passive obedience is modern and not medieval. Indeed the growth of these things is one of the factors of modern history, and one of the chief features of the age with which we are dealing. As is always the case, the growth is one of events and ideas; it is both material and moral, and it is impossible to disentangle the action and reaction of these two elements upon one another. One school of historians, or rather philosophers, fondly imagines that history is simply the working out of ideas, that political philosophy has moulded events, that force has never conquered truth, that right is might. According to this school the New Monarchy is the material result of the new ideas about kingship which spread in the fifteenth and sixteenth centuries. Another school holds that political philosophy is simply a series of deductions from past experience, of comments on facts already decided, that events have moulded ideas more than ideas have moulded events, that force is the ultimate sanction, that persecution has succeeded whenever it has been steadily and skilfully applied, that might is right. According to this school, the new ideas about kingship were simply the reflection in men's minds of the material achievements of the New Monarchy. Amid the conflict of these two schools one thing is clear, and that is that generalisations are always to some extent untrue. . . .

The correct sequence seems to be that material necessities predisposed men's minds towards a modification of the existing system; this was perceived by the rulers and statesmen of that time, who applied the practical remedy; and then followed the theoretical justification of the accomplished fact. Machiavelli did not invent his *Prince,* he merely painted him from life. Hobbes did not imagine the *Leviathan;* he merely reduced to a dogma the practice of Tudor sovereigns; and, as so often happens, the conditions, which had produced and justified that practice, had already passed away before the philosopher evolved out of it an abstract theoretical system for universal and permanent application. However that may be, the old order of the fifteenth century was in a state of liquidation, and the problem was how to keep society afloat. Every great medieval institution had gone or was going under. The empire had dissolved into nations, the prestige of the Papacy had been dimmed by its Babylonish captivity at Avignon and then by the great schism. Unity gave way to diversity of tongues, of churches, and of states; and the medieval cosmopolitan became the modern nationalist, patriot, separatist. Feudal chivalry and feudal castles had fallen before gunpowder and artillery, the growth of industry and commerce had undermined a social system based on the tenure of land; and the middle classes had sapped the power of the barons. The manorial system had broken down through the substitution of rent for services and the emancipation of the serfs. The revival of learning, the invention of the printing press, the expansion of the world by geographical discovery had removed the ancient landmarks and delivered the minds of men. There was a universal welter, a menace of general anarchy. In France the strife of Burgundian and Armagnac threatened political disintegration and the destruction of social order. The Wars of the Roses brought upon England a similar tale of disasters. Everywhere there was need of a saviour of society; everywhere this saviour was found in the king. *"Le nouveau Messie,"* says Michelet, *"est le roi."* [1]

National monarchy alone seemed to profit by the decay of other established institutions; it survived the Middle Ages and gained by their disappearance, because it was the embodiment of the coming force of nationality. Kings had already reduced the emperor, their nominal lord, to a shadow; they now made havoc with the power of their nominal subordinates, the feudal magnates; and the struggle between the disruptive forces of feudalism and the central authority ended at last in monarchical

triumph. Internal unity prepared the way for external expansion. France was first in the field. The misery and humiliation of the Hundred Years' War produced a nationalist reaction, an outburst of a new French patriotism of which Jeanne D'Arc is the inspirer and patron saint. The feud between Burgundian and Armagnac was healed; by the ordinances of Orleans (1439) the foundations were laid of a national army and a national system of finance. The cunning of Louis XI consolidated the crusade of Jeanne D'Arc. The remnants of feudal independence were crushed, and France began to expand at the cost of weaker states. Parts of Burgundy, Provence, Anjou, and Brittany were incorporated in the French monarchy; and the exuberant strength of the new-formed nation burst the barriers of the Alps, and overflowed into the plains of Italy. Other States followed the example of France; Ferdinand of Aragon married Isabella of Castile, drove out the Moors from Andalusia, and founded the modern kingdom of Spain. Marriage had been his method; but in the arts of successful matrimony none could compete with the Hapsburgs. *Bella gerant alii: tu, felix Austria, nube.* [2] Maximilian married the heiress of Charles the Bold, and united the Netherlands with Austria; his son, the Archduke Philip, married the heiress of Ferdinand of Aragon and of Isabella of Castile; and their two sons were the Emperors Charles V and Ferdinand I. The former made the Spanish Empire; the latter founded the Austro-Hungarian monarchy by wedding the daughter of the King of Hungary and Bohemia. This union, however, was purely dynastic, not national; and it was the doom of Austria to be made by the marriage of princes and marred by the discord of peoples.

The political system of Europe was thus roughly sketched out, though the boundaries of the rival kingdoms were still undetermined, and there remained minor princi-

---

[1] "The New Savior is the Monarch." [Editor's note]

[2] "Others Wage War; Thou, Happy Austria, Marry." [Editor's note]

palities and powers, chiefly in Italy and Germany, which offered an easy prey to their ambitious neighbours. For both Germany and Italy had sacrificed national unity to the shadow of universal sovereignty, Germany in the temporal and Italy in the spiritual sphere. The German king was also Holy Roman Emperor, bound by his office to the hopeless task of enforcing his authority in Italy, and Italy was the tomb of German national unity. Its own unity was prohibited by Papal ambition, for the Pope could not tolerate a secular rival in the Italian Peninsula; and, from the days of the Goth and the Lombard in the sixth and eighth centuries to those of Victor Emmanuel in the nineteenth, every aspirant for the national sovereignty of Italy has had to meet the bitter enmity of the Papacy. And so both Italy and Germany were ruled out of the national race, and had to wait three hundred years for that national consolidation which their rivals achieved in the sixteenth century.

This process of unification was not merely material and geographical. When one country is united with another it means not only a union of territory but an attempted harmony of different aspirations, interests, and politics. Look at the map of Spain, for instance. "The geography of Spain," says a recent writer on ancient history, "has always been the key to the history and even to the character of the inhabitants. Its peninsular form, and its singularly definite frontier on the one side on which it is not surrounded by the sea, give the country a superficial appearance of unity. In reality it is broken up into separate sections by a succession of transverse mountain ranges which are cut by no great river running from north to south. The dip of the country is from east to west, and accordingly the chief rivers rise near the Mediterranean and flow into the Atlantic. "Nature," it has been said by one who knew Spain well, "by thus dislocating the country, seems to have suggested localism and isolation to the inhabitants, who each in their valleys and districts are walled off from their neighbours." . . .

Each of the kingdoms, united in the fifteenth century to form Spain, had its own individual aspirations suggested by its peculiar geographical conditions. Aragon, for instance, is cut off from the rest of Spain by a series of mountain systems, and mountains are a greater barrier than the sea. It was easier to create the British Empire than to unite Germany with Italy or France with Spain. Louis XIV boasted that the Pyrenees were no more, when he placed his grandson on the Spanish throne; but the Pyrenees exist, and France and Spain are separate. Now Aragon looks towards the sea, the Mediterranean; its aspirations lie in that direction; and its Mediterranean commerce made its maritime province, Catalonia, the most progressive and the most prosperous part of Spain. There alone did a middle class and a trading population grow, and even to-day Barcelona is the headquarters of revolutionary sentiment in Spain. Instead of expanding across the mountains, it had first expanded across the sea, and had successfully laid claim to Sicily and Naples. These Mediterranean claims and ambitions, involving conflicts with France, with the Turks, and in Italy, were the contribution of Aragon to the future projects and perplexities of Spain. The dower of Castile comprised claims on Portugal and hopes of Andalusia, an oceanic sea-board with its loopholes to the New World in Vigo, La Coruña and Ferrol, and a northern outlook through Bilbao and Santander, whence Spanish trade and Spanish ships sailed the Bay of Biscay and the English Channel. Castile contributed to the United Kingdom its medieval pride and priesthood, its crusading zeal against the Moors and Indians, and the spoils of Mexico and Peru. The acquisition of Andalusia brought into the joint-stock Cadiz and Gibraltar, the command of the entrance to the Mediterranean, and African ambitions which led Charles V to waste his strength in efforts to conquer Tunis and Algiers. Union was not altogether strength; for with strength it brought distraction between conflicting ambitions and heterogeneous policies. Spain could never make up its mind on which horse to place its money, the Mediterranean, Africa, Europe, or the New World. Charles V rang the changes; now here, now there, hesitating which enterprise to take first, he could never completely succeed because he could never entirely concentrate.

France was more successful because its unity was more real. Unity in fact has been its passion under all its forms of government, and mountain chains have not secluded its people in close compartments. But its origin was as composite and its elements as varied as those of Spain. Aquitaine, which had not been peopled by the Franks, did not become really French until the seventeenth century; and the root, which Huguenotism struck in it, may have owed some of its tenacity to racial bias and the traditions of provincial independence. At any rate, before the rise of Calvinism, the south-west of France was resenting the *Gabelle* and regretting its lost connection with the English Crown. But for the most part union brought real strength to France; and the conflict between the policies, which her various acquisitions brought, was not really ruinous until the eighteenth century, when, during the Seven Years' War, she sacrificed her colonial future in pursuit of European glory. . . .

As Normandy, Brittany, and Aquitaine gave France her Atlantic position, so the acquisition of Provence brought her into the Mediterranean. . . . The partition of Burgundy by Louis XI was also a seed-plot of future strife between Valois and Hapsburg, though all the defeats of Francis I did not compel restitution. Lastly, it was the union of Anjou and Orleans with the French Crown which occasioned the French invasion of Italy, and perennial strife therein between French, Spaniards and Austrians. For, just as Aragon brought to the Spanish monarchy its claims on Naples and Sicily, so Anjou brought the competing Angevin claim to France; and

the medieval rivalry between the houses of Anjou and Aragon was merged in a more comprehensive rivalry between France and Spain. So, too, when Louis of Orleans became Louis XII of France, he endowed the French Crown with the Visconti claim to Milan, and no apple of discord produced more strife than that fertile but ill-fated duchy.

All this expansion pointed to closer contact, friendly or hostile; isolated squatters on a limitless plain or veldt have little communication; but, as soon as they have pegged out claims right up to their neighbours', they see one another more often and watch one another more closely. It was so with these national States. Hitherto diplomatic relations had been rare and spasmodic; ambassadors were only despatched on special occasions; now they became regular and resident. The necessity of watching one another's designs begat the modern diplomatic system; mutual adjustment of each other's disputes produced international law —an incomprehensible idea when all States were theoretically subject to one imperial suzerain; and mutual jealousy of each other's growth gave rise to the theory of the balance of power.

The external development of the area, over which the national monarch ruled, reacted upon the degree of authority which he exercised within his dominions. Every extension of his sway intensified his dignity and power, and lifted him higher above his subjects. Local liberties and feudal rights, which checked a Duke of Brittany or King of Aragon, were powerless against a King of France or a King of Spain.

The circumstances of which we have been speaking in connection with the New Monarchy were anything but favourable to the development of Parliamentary independence and prestige. Indeed, everywhere but in England Parliamentary institutions almost disappeared. The States-General met for the last time in France before the revolution in 1614; the Cortes of the Spanish Peninsula grew insignificant. In Germany the Imperial Diet and the provincial assemblies lost much of their influence, and ceased to control the territorial princes. The same tendencies threatened the future of the Houses of Lords and Commons. Parliament in the sixteenth century seemed to meet only to register the monarch's decrees and to clothe with a legal cloak the naked despotism of his acts. . . . The sphere of royal authority encroached upon all others; all functions and all powers tended to concentrate in royal hands. The king was the emblem of national unity, the centre of national aspirations, and the object of national reverence. In France and Spain men had many provincial parliaments, but they had only one king.

This monarch gained as much from the growth of the new ideas as he did from the decay of the old. The Renaissance, the revived study of Roman Civil Law, and the Reformation itself all contributed to the growth of royal absolutism. There seems no direct connection between the study of Greek and political despotism; but indirectly the passion for scholarship took the zest out of politics. Moreover, scholars who worked with their pens had to live on their pensions; and pensions are more easily got from princes than from parliaments. Parliaments will vote huge sums to successful generals, but never a penny to a great scholar or sculptor, poet or painter; for purely intellectual achievements are not as yet regarded as services to the State. And so the host of Renaissance scholars looked to the king and were not disappointed; every New Monarch was in his way a new Mæcenas, and had his reward in the praise of the world of letters, which found as little to say for parliaments as parliaments found to give.

The Renaissance did a more direct service to the New Monarchy. Men turned not only to the theology, literature and art of the early Christian era; they also began to study anew its political organisation and its system of law and jurisprudence. The code of Justinian was as much a revelation as the original Greek of the New Testament. Roman Imperial Law seemed as superior to the barbarities of common law and feudal custom as classical did to medieval Latin. England escaped with a comparatively mild attack of Roman law, because she had early been inoculated with it under Henry II. But the attack proved fatal to maturer constitutions; and Roman Civil Law supplanted indigenous systems in France and Germany, in the Netherlands, Spain and Scotland. Nothing could have suited the kings of the New Monarchy better; common law, canon law, and feudal custom were all of them checks upon despotism. The Roman Civil Law could be used against all; *quod principi placuit legis habet vigorem*[3] ran the maxim of Ulpian, a maxim which could be quoted against Popes as well as against parliaments. Nor was this all; Roman emperors were habitually deified, and men in the sixteenth century were almost inclined to pay similar honours to their kings.

The Reformation itself encouraged this tendency of the Renaissance; and there is no greater error than to think that that movement had anything to do with political liberty. Protestantism, it is true, was originally an appeal to private judgment against authority, but only in spiritual matters. Luther explained to the rebellious peasants of Germany that the Gospel message of freedom for all mankind was not an attack on serfdom; and even in the spiritual sphere the Reformers soon fell into the error of the French Revolutionists when they announced their intention of compelling men to be free. All believed in fire as the proper purge of heresy; they only differed about the heresy and about the rival rights of Church and State to prescribe the fire. They claimed national independence of Rome, but repudiated individual right to dissent from the national Church or the national State. For the State they asserted, if not infallibility, at any rate divine institution and unlimited authority to enforce its will. They proclaimed a right of resistance to the Church and a duty of passive

[3] "Whatever pleases the Prince has the force of Law." [Editor's note]

obedience to the State. They reverted in fact to the political theory of the primitive Church; it was part of the Renaissance, the revival of the ancient, and repudiation of the medieval. Now the primitive Church had a simple political theory, which was not by any means original. The writers of the New Testament and the Fathers of the Church were born into the conditions of a despotic system. They accepted it just as they accepted slavery, not as good things in themselves but as a divinely ordained remedy or punishment for the original sin of man. The powers that be are ordained of God, said St. Paul; and working on this basis, some of the Fathers developed the theory that the person and authority of the ruler were so sacred that resistance to him was equivalent to resistance to God Himself. This was the idea borrowed by the Reformers. . . . The Reformers, like some early Fathers, transferred the divine authority of the State, whole and entire, to the particular ruler. Circumstances required a saviour of society and the Reformation consecrated him. "The new Messiah is the king."

Nowhere was the king more emphatically the saviour of society than in England. The sixty years of Lancastrian rule were in the seventeenth century represented as the golden age of parliamentary government, a sort of time before the fall to which popular orators appealed against the Stuart despotism. The Lancastrian kings were at the mercy of their parliaments, and parliament in the seventeenth century wished to do the same by the Stuarts; that was their idea of government. But to keen observers of the time the chief characteristic of Lancastrian rule was its "lack of governance," or administrative anarchy. The limitations of parliament were never more striking than when its power stood highest. Even in the sphere of legislation, the Statute Book has seldom been so barren. Its principal acts were to narrow the county electorate to an oligarchy by restricting the franchise to forty-shilling freeholders, excluding leaseholders and copy-

holders altogether; and to confine the choice of electors to local men. It was not content with legislative authority; it interfered with the executive, which it could hamper but could not control. It was possessed with the inveterate fallacy that freedom and strong government are things incompatible, that the executive is the natural enemy of the legislature, that if one is strong the other must be weak. It preferred a weak executive, and strove to compel the king to "live of his own," when "his own" was absolutely inadequate to meet the barest necessities of administration. It failed to realise that liberty without order is licence; that order must be established before liberty can be enjoyed; and that a strong government is the only means of enforcing order. Parliament had acquired power, but repudiated responsibility; and the connecting link between it and the Crown had yet to be found in the Cabinet. Hence the Lancastrian experiment ended in a generation of civil war, and the memory of that anarchy explains much of the Tudor despotism.

The problems of sixteenth-century history can only be solved by realising the misrule of the previous age, the failure of parliamentary government, and the strength of the popular demand for a firm and masterful hand at the wheel. . . .

So it was in sixteenth-century England. Parliament had been tried and found wanting. "A plague on both your Houses" was the cry; and both Houses passed out of the range of popular imagination and almost out of the sphere of independent political action. Men were tired of politics; they wanted peace, peace to pursue new avenues of wealth, to study new problems of literature, art, and religion.

They cared little for parliamentary principles, and vastly preferred that the king should levy benevolences from the rich, than that Parliament should impose taxes on the poor. . . . The men of that day needed no charm against a monarch who embodied national aspirations and voiced the national will. References to the Charter are as rare in the debates of Parliament as

they are in the pages of Shakespeare. Not
till the Stuarts came was Magna Carta discovered; and the best-hated instruments of
Stuart tyranny were popular institutions
under the Tudors. . . . England in the
sixteenth century put its trust in its princes
far more than it did in its Parliaments. It
invested them with attributes almost divine;
no one but a Tudor poet would ever have
thought of the "Divinity that doth hedge
a king"; or have written: —

> Not all the water in the rough, rude sea,
> Can wash the balm off from an anointed
>   king.
> The breath of worldly men cannot depose
> The deputy elected by the Lord.

"Love for the King," wrote a Venetian of
Henry VIII in his early years, "is universal
with all who see him; for his Highness
does not seem a person of this world, but
one descended from Heaven." The new
Messiah is the king.

Such were the tendencies which the
kings of the New Monarchy crystallised
into practical weapons of absolute government. Royalty had become a caste apart.
. . . To them [the subjects] there was
nothing strange in the union of Church
and State, and in the supremacy of the
king over both: for, while they professed
Christianity in various forms, the State was
their real religion, and the king was their
Great High Priest. They were consumed
with the idea that the State was the end
and crown of human endeavour; it was
their idol and their ideal. It inspired them,
and they became its slaves. This is the real
tyranny of Tudor times; individual life,
liberty, and conscience were as nothing
compared with national interests. Nationalism was young, presumptuous, and exigent;
its passion had no patience with the foes to
its desires, and its cruelty was only equalled
by its vigour. The New Monarchy was the
emblem and the focus of these forces; it
had a great and an indispensable part to
play in the making of modern England; it
was strong, unprincipled, and efficient. But
its greatest achievement was that its success
made the reception of such an experiment
superfluous for the future. Order is Heav-
en's first law; on earth it must always go
before liberty. . . . Moral and political
principles are the slow and painful achievement of ages: and you can no more judge
the New Monarchy by the standards of
to-day, than you can apply to the child the
canons by which you approve or condemn
the adult. To use the same test for the sixteenth and twentieth centuries is to imply
that man stands to-day where he did then,
and to ignore the progress of four hundred
years.

VARIATIONS ON THE MAIN THEME

ROLAND MOUSNIER

Professor Mousnier was born in 1907. His entire academic life has been spent in research, writing and teaching connected with the period from ca. 1500–1750. His many distinguished contributions include his ground-breaking study, *La Vénalité*, a basic study of the connection between the sale of offices and the growth of royal government. In addition to numerous other books and articles, Mousnier has been very active in the work of the International Congress of the Historical Sciences.

THE CONDITIONS OF ABSOLUTE MONARCHY'S PROGRESS

In the sixteenth century the majority of the European States were evolving towards absolute monarchy. Absolute monarchy exists when the king, embodying the national ideal, possesses in addition, in law as well as in fact, the attributes of sovereignty: the power to make laws, to dispense justice, to levy taxes, to maintain a permanent army, to appoint officials, to decide what constitutes attacks against the public welfare, and, in particular, against the royal authority, by virtue of his extraordinary jurisdiction arising from his power as the fountain of justice. The idea of absolute monarchy is added to the old ideas of contract and of custom regulating the relations of kings with their vassals and their subjects. It does not destroy the old ideas, but is tempered by them.

These great states were moreover activated and unified by a powerful patriotism, which mixed strangely with local patriotism and with the feeling of fidelity toward the local suzerain. This broader patriotism, although very ancient, blossomed by virtue of great foreign struggles, which created an awareness of common interests by the action of the royal officials as a result of new economic relations; and, even more, because of the influence of the humanists on the courtiers and the great bourgeois leaders who gave a tone to society. Humanism gave to this sentiment, which sprang from the innermost depths of the individual and from the reaction of man to his homeland, supplementary characteristics: clarity, precision, form. As a result royal power increased. In France, the humanist Budé felt that his country was animated by a collective soul; that it was a person; and he dedicated his treatise *De Asse* to the *"Genie de la France."* [1] The French humanists proclaimed the superiority of France. Gaguin,[2] driven by love of this native land, his "mother," enumerated the virtues particularly French — chivalrous gallantry, the love of work and of thrift, a sweetness of life, gentleness of manners. Valeran de Valerannes[3] demonstrated that

[1] Budé wrote his *De Asse et partibus eius* in 1515. It was a store of information on classical antiquity, although its subject ostensibly was Roman coinage. The dedication was to "the tutelary spirit of France." [Editor's note]
[2] Robert Gaguin was labelled the "general" of the Parisian humanists by the great historian Huizinga, obviously in reference to the fact that he was the General of the Order of Mathurins or Trinitarians. His love of France was expressed in his Latin textbook history, *De origine et gestis Francorum Compendium* (1495). [Editor's note]
[3] The French humanistic historian. [Editor's note]

From Roland Mousnier, *Histoire générale des Civilisations: Les XVIe et XVIIe Siècles* (Paris, 1961), pp. 108–109, 112–116. Reprinted by permission of the Presses Universitaires de France. Translated by the editor, with the assistance of Carolyn Scales.

France was the head of the family of nations. The Gauls had conquered Greece, Ionia, Macedonia, had taken Rome, and civilized the Cisalpine world; while their descendants had subdued Germany, delivered the Papacy, and liberated the Orient from the Infidels. And in these conquests, France, the missionary bearer of ideas, had always remained faithful to her spirit of unselfishness and of idealism.

Even England had celebrated the victory of Charles Martel over the Saracens, because in that struggle Europe received liberty as a gift of the French. The French had become imbued with these ideas. They were informed and illuminated by the history of profound, eternal sentiments, which allowed the idea of the Christian knight to change into that of classical patriotism. [An example may be given]. Francis I had just learned from Galiot de Genouillac, his captain-general of artillery, of the death of Galiot's son who was killed at Cerisoles. Galiot says simply: "I thank you, my God, for this son whom you gave me, when it pleased you, you have taken him back from me." And turning to the king: "I rejoice, sir, to have had this son who has died courageously *for you and for the country*." Now Galiot was interested in ancient culture and his son had a humanist tutor.

Castilians, English, Flemish, however, were in no way second to the French in this respect. In Italy, the Venetians, the Florentines and the Neapolitan nation, as well as humanists like Machiavelli, sought by their writing to advance the unity and the independence of Italy. In the multiple nations of the Holy Empire, the humanists, like Wympheling of Strasbourg, kept alive the ideal of German unity. And this patriotism attained the proportions of what we would call nationalism.

The progress of absolute monarchy, however, was not due solely to the natural desire of kings to increase their power. By the thirteenth century the revival of Roman law had already recovered the notion of the absolute prince, who concentrated all power in his person and whose will was law. The vogue of antiquity gave a new surge to the Roman law in the sixteenth century and added to it the ancient idea of the "hero" — the demi-god, dominating and beneficent. But it was not only these cultural ideals which imposed themselves on the individual and thenceforth determined his actions. The Roman law owed its success to the fact that it provided a convenient mode of expression for deep-seated tendencies of the time. The hero was the model of a being to whom the peoples yearned to surrender themselves. The doctrine of absolutism answered the dominant needs of Renaissance society and appeared to be a need of the whole social body. The necessity of a strong power was imposed also at first by the prevalence of foreign wars. With the establishment of great political units, strong enough so that their leaders were no longer totally absorbed by internecine struggles and were able to devote themselves to extending their power outwards, with the progress of those States towards the establishment of economic unity, began the great wars for economic and political hegemony. War necessitated the strengthening of authority and the existence of governments capable of making rapid decisions, promptly and universally executed.

The necessity of a strong power stemmed also from the very composition of the nations. They were a juxtaposition of territorial communities, provinces, counties, municipalities, village communities, and corporate bodies, e.g., the orders: the clergy, the nobility, and Third Estate; also the corps of officers, the universities, the trade guilds. The monarchies made agreements, first with one group and then with another. Each community, each order, had its privileges, its customs, its rulings, its immunities, its jurisdiction, its assets, its leaders, its representatives, and was a force to be heeded. Corporate bodies and communities were unceasingly at war among themselves by virtue of their particular interests. The king had to be strong enough to arbitrate their conflicts and coordinate their individual pursuits in the light of the common good. Indeed, their divisions often gave him the opportunity to pursue a policy of "divide and conquer."

The same holds true for the rivalries of the great seigniorial families — the Eboli and the Alba in Spain; the Chalons, the Vergez, the Horn and the Egmont in the Low Countries and in Franche-Comté; the Bourbons, the Montmorencys, the Guises and the Condés in France, etc. They were dangerous because of the survival of certain feelings and practices from the Middle Ages. The ties of vassalage created for the seigniorial leaders elaborate *clienteles,* supporters, groups of dependents — men ready to kill and even to commit treason for their lords. Family ties worked in the same fashion. They were so strong that marrying a distant cousin of a great lord was a way of assuring for oneself forever the favor and protection of that nobleman. But, in return, one took a vow to serve him, even against the king. Thus the king found revolving around the great families vast clamlike groups. But he, in his turn, had his own *clientele* of faithful and devoted vassals over against those of potential rebels. He found it easy to secure the adherence of the rivals of a traitor.

Finally, absolute monarchy resulted from the antagonism of two classes, the bourgeoisie and the nobility. The king needed the bourgeois for his finances, and easily obtained their obedience or their support. The royal power enriched the bourgeois merchants by its borrowing, by the mortgaging of crown lands, by the farming out of royal taxes, by the granting of exploitative monopolies, by giving protection against the laws of the Church on usury and against seigniorial burdens, as well as against the corporations. The royal power saved the masters of trade by giving legal status and judicial protection to their corporations, and by thus defending their *clientele* and their revenues against the alien capitalists. The crown also protected the bourgeois merchants and craftsmen against the new proletariat.

The dream of members of the bourgeois class was to raise themselves to noble rank. But only the king was able to thus advance them and facilitate this change of social class, by conferring upon them ennobling public offices, by gratifying them with bishoprics and abbeys, by bestowing upon them patents of nobility, by permitting them to hold noble fiefs. The bourgeois passed into the nobility, and, in this sense, one can say that the bourgeoisie became aristocratic. But these ennobled merchants kept their bourgeois habits of ruthless appetite for gain, of economy, of calculating prudence. Perrenot, Count of Granvelle, Bishop of Arras, Chancellor of the Empire, was a good instance. Even in the most critical moments, insofar as his own policy and that of the Emperor his master was concerned, he glossed the long statements sent by his stewards on the wheat crops and the state of the market; he decided himself the opportune time for selling produce; and always anticipated events with more skill than did his servants. He sent four-page letters on the precautions to be taken in order to prevent the loss of a small inheritance in mortmain; when no artisans could be obtained to do the work, he prepared letters on the conditions of various furs . . . and even refused to permit anyone to dispense bread and butter without his explicit warrant. In this sense, then, the nobility also became bourgeois. If, however, some of the old nobility adopted similar habits, if such customs crept into ancient families *via* wives of bourgeois origin, on the whole there were two nobilities: the old nobility of the sword, scornful and haughty; and the new nobility, which managed only in the course of time, laboriously, and after many of its members turned to soldiering to obtain recognition as "quality."

The nobility was unable to defend itself against the bourgeoisie, except by the favor of the king. In general, they practiced only the profession of arms, neglected their lands and their feudal rights. Besides, the depreciation of money decreased their incomes, based largely in fixed rents. Of course the nobility could still live on its lands, content with rentals in kind and the labor services of the peasants. But the royal courts, the salons and clubs of the cities, the far-away expeditions, attracted them. It ruined itself at these pastimes, all the more so since luxury was a seigniorial obligation. Giving handsome presents, *largesse,* was a noble tradition that become more and more burdensome. Yet the rise of the bourgeoisie made it even more necessary, by some Nietzschean sentiment, to preserve as virtues even the worst faults of the nobility, if they were to distinguish themselves from the merchants. The noble houses maintained an army of servants, maids and valets. Weddings were an occasion for dances, tournaments, ballets and other costly spectacles. Funerals called for hundreds of masses, special funeral chambers, processions of the poor dressed in mourning, widows and orphans carrying candles, alms which ate up the equivalent of the annual income of a good bourgeois family. At a Court Ball, they bedecked themselves lavishly and extravagantly. Thus the nobleman was obliged to enter the service of the king, to solicit, according to his rank, the government of a province or of a fortified town, a regiment, company, or even an ordinary place in the artillery. He might solicit pensions, gifts for the marriages of his children, even abbeys and bishoprics for his younger sons. Against the rising bourgeoisie, the nobleman's only defense of his effective rank in society was by recourse to the king. In truth, at least in Europe west of the Elbe and the Dinaric Alps, there were fewer and fewer independent feudal lords, an ever diminishing number of seigniors exercising public power in their domains, contingent only on fidelity to their suzerain. In their place we find an ever-growing *noblesse,* a greater mass of social groups to whom the head of state gave superior status in society, with an hereditary title, in exchange for their military service and their work in government. That superior hereditary right carried with it hierarchical titles (dukes, marquis, counts, barons, etc.), marks of honor and distinctions, as well as a means of existence. All came to depend on the State.

This struggle of the classes was perhaps the principal factor in the development of absolute monarchies.

Paradoxically, these absolute monarchies had, however, less effective power, less real influence on the daily life of each of their subjects than even the liberal democratic governments of the nineteenth century. The Christian divine law; the fundamental laws of the realm which expressed certain conditions of existence; the laws protecting certain rights like those which secured property, corporations and communities, their contracts, customs and privileges; all that limited the power of the king. He was limited also by the small number of royal officials, as well as by the difficulty of communications. To confine ourselves to the civil officers, in France where the *king* had at his disposal the most numerous corps of officers in Europe, this number did not exceed, in the year 1505, 12,000 for about 15 million inhabitants or one official for every forty square kilometers. (In 1934, in a much more complex society, the figures are 1 to every 70 inhabitants and 56 for every 40 sq. kilometers.) The authority of the central government was exercised, but much less frequently and less continuously and effectively than now. Many of the functions which in modern times devolve upon the state were then performed by members of the nobility, acting in seigniorial capacities, or by corporations and other organized groups.

The principle of absolutism did in fact permit the co-existence of unofficial groups of diverse kinds at a period in their history when their very survival was at stake. There was always an admixture of the idea of contract and custom, thus obviating the excesses present at the time of . . . Justinian. The composite idea permitted the realization of a balance between excessive conditions of dispersion and of division; it facilitated, in the midst of struggles, the continued existence of kingdoms and allowed them to move toward a more centralized and more unified type of State which was to be so necessary for further progress.

THE "NEW MONARCHY" AND TUDOR GOVERNMENT

WALTER CECIL RICHARDSON

Professor Richardson has spent the major portion of his academic life at Louisiana State University, where he currently serves as Boyd Professor of History. He has done pioneer work in English constitutional and administrative history. In addition to his study of Chamber Administration, which received the Herbert Baxter Adams Prize, he is the author of numerous articles, as well as *The History of the Court of Augmentations* and *Stephen Vaughan*. He is currently at work on a history of the Inns of Court.

THE victory of Henry Tudor at Bosworth Field on August 22, 1485, ushered in a new order as well as a "new monarchy." By a quiet and unspectacular aggrandizement of power, the Tudors achieved a complete royal supremacy which their predecessors, during centuries of struggle with the baronage, had failed to attain. Yet this concentration of power in the hands of the sovereign effected no abrupt changes in either constitutional forms or procedures. The "newness" of the Tudor rule lay, not in any novelty of the governmental system, but in the thoroughness with which it was administered. Old institutions were invigorated and adapted to new uses, while newer agencies followed the traditional pattern of well-established precedent. Though numerous innovations were introduced, they did not materially disrupt the essential continuity of fifteenth-century administration; rather, the newer agencies and improved administrative techniques served to strengthen the principle of conciliar government. The success of the administration rested primarily upon the efficiency of its personnel and the tireless supervision of capable royal ministers, under the personal direction of king and council.

In the long history of feudal England it has become customary to regard the reign of Henry VII as the breaking point between medievalism and the rise of the national state. This notion carries with it the convenient corollary that the sixteenth century witnessed the final collapse of the system of manorial economy in the dawn of a modern era. Such an interpretation, however, overemphasizes the transitional nature of the period. Despite the renaissance ideals of wealth, power, and efficiency, the basic concepts of government were medieval. Not only in estate manage-

From Walter Cecil Richardson, *Tudor Chamber Administration, 1485–1547* (Baton Rouge, La., 1952), pp. 1–2, 5, 9–10, 29–31, 443–449. Reprinted by permission of the Louisiana State University Press.

ment but in the entire field of administration, the Tudor monarchy bore a strong resemblance to the rule of a powerful medieval suzerain. The king was still a feudal lord in his own right, with a power and a prerogative jurisdiction that were practically unlimited. His revenues from the vast demesne lands were far greater than the revenues of any English sovereign preceding him, and his rights of patronage were those of king and suzerain combined. Tenants *in capite* still carried the burdens of feudal incidents and feudal tenure. These and other vestiges of feudal practices persisted far into the seventeenth century, long after the formal system of feudalism had disintegrated.

Social and economic changes, in progress for half a century, gained momentum after the close of the Wars of the Roses. Although the transformation was not immediately apparent, the strong Tudor rule had the effect of accelerating the movement. A vigorous foreign policy restored public confidence in national leadership, which in the council as in the broader field of public administration was everywhere recruited from the ranks of the rising middle classes. Foreign alliances, commercial treaties, and a controlled domestic economy proved a strong impetus to both trade and industry. Throughout the entire orbit of national life, as in the broader cultural and economic spheres, the pulse of the nation quickened. As baronial influence and immunity waned, the rigidity of older institutions gradually gave way to the flexibility of the new. By the beginning of the reign of Henry VIII the basic principles of the Tudor system of government were fully developed. The ensuing changes of the sixteenth century were largely an outgrowth of the earlier reforms, which had clearly outlined the policies of the future.

*   *   *

In 1485 lack of good government, over which there was so much murmuring, was prevalent all over the realm, but certainly such popular complaint was not new. The entire century had been filled with wars, disorders, rebellions, low morality, and a maladministration of justice. The later civil was had only rendered the necessity for reform more acute. The country was sadly in need of a respite from war and internal dissension, of a period of peace in which to turn her energies to the task of domestic reconstruction. Under Richard III honesty and efficiency in government had been all but forgotten. If reforms were to be effective, a new and invigorated administration was necessary, one whose personnel would put the interest of their king before the temptations of personal ends or individual profit. Henry's goal was to set the crown supreme over all rival interests; to put loyalty beyond greed, efficiency above the decadence of overorganized medieval institutionalism. The supremacy of monarchy must no longer be questioned. With the power of purse and prerogative right it was soon to become a fact.

*   *   *

Once the nobility had been brought under royal control, the real test of Tudor security was financial independence. In conformity with traditional theory and practice the king was expected to "live of his own," without recourse to parliament for normal supplies. Although parliamentary assessments were commonly resorted to for extraordinary expenses, such expedients were slow and unpopular. Consequently the English sovereigns had devised all sorts of extraneous means of raising money within the constitutional limits imposed upon their royal prerogative. Despite the fact that it had become increasingly difficult to meet all the ordinary expenses out of the declining crown revenues, it was still an accepted mark of good government to do so. Henry Tudor's earlier efforts to improve his financial position eventually determined the twofold revenue policy of the reign: an extension of the ordinary revenues, whereby the royal income was tremendously increased, and the frugal husbanding of his own resources. By the time these ends were attained, he had set up a new chamber machinery to assist the older exchequer in the control of the enlarged revenue administration.

The ordinary revenues of the crown were derived chiefly from the hereditary royal estates, which constituted the "ancient demesne." As late as the sixteenth century all the revenues derived from the royal lands were considered a part of the ordinary revenues that had "subsisted time out of mind in the crown." Blackstone classified them as a branch of the "ordinary" revenues of the kingdom, as differentiated from the "extraordinary" revenues, by which the regular hereditary patrimony of the crown was supplemented from time to time. The latter included the usual parliamentary subsidies, customs, grants, and special aids. Taken collectively, all the revenues may be regarded as the king's fiscal prerogative, which, though greatly enlarged in the sixteenth century, remained essentially unaltered in nature during the entire Tudor period. The later distinction between that which was the king's, in his public as contrasted with his private capacity, was unknown, the theoretical idea of kingship not yet having developed. "Crown lands" and "the king's lands" were synonymous terms. Likewise, whatever was the nation's was the king's, to be employed to his personal profit and advantage if he so desired. Since the crown demesne was the principal source of the king's recurrent income, it is not surprising that Henry VII seized every opportunity to extend his territorial possessions.

*   *   *

Throughout the Middle Ages the king's household, with its offshoots, the exchequer, chancery, chamber, and wardrobe, was the central agency for the direction of all departments of English administration. The exchequer and the chancery, gradually freeing themselves from the control of the household, went "out of court" and developed into independent national institutions. The wardrobe and the chamber,

however, continued as integral divisions of the household, carrying on the executive work formerly performed by the older *curia regis*. During the fourteenth century these two departments of the court were continually encroaching upon the jurisdiction of the chancery and the exchequer. Under the personal control of the king, subject to his supervision and staffed by his own servants, both wardrobe and chamber could be used as royal agencies to offset the growing power of parliament. In resisting baronial attempts to control all household offices the crown resorted to the expedient of developing, first, the wardrobe and, later, the chamber, in an effort to retain an independent household administration.

The financial independence of the crown required the king to retain a more direct control of his revenues than was normally afforded him under the traditional revenue system. Since all revenues were normally paid into the exchequer, it was necessary to secure an order from that body for all expenditures, both national and personal. The king, therefore, was not only dependent upon parliament for necessary revenues to meet the running expenses of government but was also forced to rely upon the exchequer for a final collection and eventual distribution to the household departments. This procedure was at once inconvenient and inefficient. The traditional processes of the medieval exchequer were proverbially slow and rigid. The king found it more desirable to divert, when possible, particular revenues from their normal exchequer course to the more personalized administration of the elastic household departments. As early as the reign of Edward I the wardrobe had become a rival treasury which received and spent the national income. The exchequer continued to collect the assigned revenues paid to the wardrobe, but it gradually gave up the administration and distribution of funds.

In the long struggle between the barons and the crown, Edward II, Edward IV, and Richard III resorted to a similar strategy, by which they secured a measure of independence from the close financial supervision of parliament. As the wardrobe and, later, the chamber were expanded into domestic treasuries, they functioned as practical disbursing departments of the household. Consequently the transfer of the collection of revenues and the auditing of accounts from the exchequer to a domestic treasury was a logical development. Although such earlier innovations were, at times, temporarily successful, the exchequer always managed eventually to regain its original administrative and jurisdictional authority. Royal control or finance through the household departments, therefore, was but a temporary expedient. Such measures were resorted to only when the crown was strong enough to defy parliament openly, and they never became a constitutional part of the national system. Until a thorough reform of the entire government was effected, there was little chance that the strongly entrenched exchequer would relinquish its traditional hold upon the royal purse. Such a contingency arose, however, after the anarchy of the fifteenth century had caused a general decay of all governmental administration. The Tudor monarchy took advantage of the opportunity by reintroducing a modified chamber system, which ultimately deprived the exchequer of its practical control of crown revenues. The changes were begun by Henry VII, in whose reign a new chapter in the history of English revenue administration was inaugurated.

*   *   *

Within the framework of Tudor absolutism the chamber system was fashioned to fulfill the needs of a strong, centralized monarchy. Among the many objectives to be realized, the accumulation of a large reserve of capital became a dominant factor in the new program. The expenses of Tudor adventuring in European politics, as well as the rising costs of domestic administration, emphasized the need for a full treasury, but the real problem was one of finding new sources of income. The solution was discovered in two main revenue expedients, the revival of feudal assessments and the extension of the demesne holdings of the crown. In an effort to achieve financial independence, Henry VII resorted to nonparliamentary devices for raising money. At the same time, the revival of old, established rights and royal privileges enabled him to maintain that extraordinary prerogative power which made his son and successor famous. By the turn of the sixteenth century, profits from confiscated property, feudal levies, arbitrary fines, and revived feudal incidents were accepted as regular sources of revenue derived from prerogative jurisdiction.

Incidental to the development of that prerogative was the gradual acquisition of an enlarged crown demesne. As the royal estates multiplied in number, they were put under the control of the chamber organization, which in turn was expanded to meet the increased demands made upon it. Departments were enlarged or reconstituted, while gradually new offices were added to supervise the several prerogative functions and collect the nonrecurrent revenues that were channeled through the chamber treasury. In time the chamber was fully departmentalized by Henry VIII, who used it as the chief medium of finance for both domestic and foreign affairs. Since the revenues grew steadily, various supervisory institutions were erected to accommodate the expanding administration. Older offices were enlarged into statutory courts of record and new departments created to bolster up the improvised system. These newer agencies, particularly the court of augmentations, at once encroached upon the jurisdiction of the chamber and the older courts of common law. Before the close of the reign of Henry VIII, the chamber organization had lost its original simplicity. In the broader scheme of revenue control the more personalized direction of the king and council had given way to a complex, bureaucratic regulation through the five great financial courts of the realm, that operated more or less independently of each other. Gradually the chamber system disintegrated, as the court of augmentations came to dominate the entire economic structure. . . .

Whatever the internal weaknesses of the system, the more practical objectives of over half a century of careful planning had been realized. The permanent revenues from crown lands had been greatly augmented by an unprecedented enlargement of the ancient demesne. Numerous prerogative devices, designed to tap new sources of supply, had resulted in an extraordinary increase in the temporary revenues. Not only had the newer crown agencies and revenue courts brought the collection and expenditure of revenues more directly under the control of the crown and council; they also had improved the administration. Instead of all the finances of the kingdom being administered, as formerly, through a single institution, the national exchequer, they had been apportioned among a number of quasi-independent departments: the exchequer, the duchy chamber, the first fruits and tenths, the wards and liveries, the general surveyors, and the augmentations. Henry VII had achieved a personal financial independence through his chamber, which Henry VIII used in the dual capacity of private treasury and a department of state finance. After departmentalization, when the chamber system grew too complex to meet his more personalized needs, the king established his own privy purse, under the direct control of some one of the trusted household servants. Thus, within the expanding financial organization, the principle of royal independence was preserved.

Although the possibilities of corruption were inherent in the system, it operated successfully as long as the guiding hand of the sovereign was strong enough to hold the ambitious ministers in check. Despite the tendency toward overorganization the bureaucracy was, in function, direct and practical. When stripped of technical terminology and legal formalism, the offices and institutions were exceedingly simple. In an age when political theory was subservient to practical efficiency, the kingly power was translated into administrative procedures that the commonest subject could use and understand.

*   *   *

Within the scope of chamber administration, feudal principles and medieval forms persisted throughout the Tudor period. While significant changes were introduced, they were not regarded by contemporaries as innovative. In husbandry, in the maintenance of revenue control, and in general administration, old customs and well-established feudatory rights were sustained. New policies were formulated, but ancient laws and traditional practices were preserved. Even in the religious settlement there was a striking continuity of medieval forms. The royal prerogative in the state, however applicable to changing conditions, was still grounded in the feudal structure of the Middle Ages. This continuity of institutional form and pattern persisted long after the chamber system had sunk into oblivion. . . .

In all other aspects the basic principles of personal rule carried over into the seventeenth century. The Stuarts, like the Tudors, were forced to accept the medieval notion that the king should live of his own. The alternative was a surrender of all the prerogative gains of the past century and an acceptance of subservience to a resentful parliament, which was becoming more and more expressive of the national will. It is significant that the main issue in the struggle between the Stuarts and parliament was a financial one, centering in a dispute over questions of taxation and prerogative assessments. Fundamentally, the problem of the financial independence of the crown was even greater in the seventeenth than in the sixteenth century, because of the increased costs of administration and national defense. Furthermore, there were no new sources of income to add to the impoverished inheritance. The ingenious Tudors had exploited them all and in some instances, as in the case of the wealth of the church, had exhausted the possibilities of further increment. The high-handed policy of the Stuarts was born not so much from stubbornness and pride as from actual need. If the Tudors had husbanded their resources instead of dissipating them, had considered their extensive acquisitions of land and property as capital to be invested instead of income to be spent, the revenue controversy might have been postponed for another century. Typical of the response of the crown to the prevailing circumstances of each period was the problem of the sale of crown lands and timber. A policy begun in recklessness ended in necessity.

The early Stuarts were not unmindful of their legacy in the field of prerogative jurisdiction. If a justification in usage was necessary, convenient precedents, both recent and well established, were at hand. In their exercise of prerogative functions, the Stuarts simply maintained that royal authority so uniquely wielded by the Tudors, which John Cowell defined in *The Interpreter* as the "especial power, pre-eminence or privilege that the king hath above the ordinary course of the common law." All the Tudor devices were employed: monopolies, impositions, purveyance, wardship, marriage, attainder, forfeiture, primer seisin, livery, ouster le main, relief, escheat, distraint of knighthood, and irregular fines imposed by right of an indivisible sovereignty which was converted by James I into an "absolute" prerogative. In this respect there was no significant break with the past. James told his parliament in 1610 that he would tolerate no infringement upon those prerogative rights received from his predecessors. "Such things I would be sorry should be accounted for grievances," he declared,

"for I would be loath to be quarrelled in my ancient rights and possessions; for that were to judge me unworthy of that which my predecessors had and left me."

On the other hand, the Tudors, unlike their less tactful successors, had never attempted to set royal authority above the needs of the body politic. Nor had they defied the will of parliament by the insistence upon doctrinal justification of prerogative right. Practical absolutism was grounded in constitutional forms and based upon the principle of rule through parliament. At no time was the validity of parliamentary authority questioned. Rather, the Tudors furthered the development of the house of commons by stimulating a more active participation of the middle classes in national legislation. The unbroken continuity of parliamentary development and the consolidation of parliamentary gains was no less a major achievement of the sixteenth century than the institutional changes effected in the general administration. That the Tudors might have attained their objectives by royal fiat, without the support of parliament, is but a reflection of the confidence imposed in them; nonetheless, they seldom found it necessary to resort to that extremity. The very fact that recently all the instruments of arbitrary government had been tried and tested in the cauldron of political expediency led to their ultimate rejection. As the needs for a strong monarchy receded, the resistance to royal supremacy increased. Successful parliamentary opposition had already emerged during the closing years of the Elizabethan period. The revolt against personal rule, terminating in the later struggle between king and parliament, as well as the repudiation of the last vestiges of feudal survivals, was an outgrowth of the Tudor regime.

THE TUDOR REVOLUTION:
THE MODERN STATE IS FORMED

G. R. ELTON

Dr. Elton was born in 1921. After leaving Prague as a young man he was educated in England, taking a Ph.D. in History at University College, London. Since 1948 he has established himself as a leading authority on the Tudor period, especially on constitutional problems and the Reformation era. Currently a Fellow of Clare College, Cambridge, he has been since 1954 University Lecturer in History. Among his most important works are numerous articles and several books, the most distinguished being his *England Under the Tudors* and also *The Tudor Constitution*.

THERE have been periods when the needs of "good government" prevailed over the demands of "free government," and of these the Tudor age was the most important. To speak of despotism and a reign of terror in sixteenth-century England was easier for a generation which had not met these things at first hand; however, it remains true that it was a time when men were ready to be governed, and when order and peace seemed more important than principles and rights. What distinguished the Tudors from their European contemporaries, who were facing similar problems, was just that they provided peace and order without despotism — certainly without the weapons of the despot. One would think, therefore, that the history of Tudor government ought to be well known. Up to a point it is the place of the justice of the peace, the role of the privy council, even to some extent the part played by parliament: these are supposedly well established. But the methods and machinery of central government have received little attention. There is no series of monographs such as — grouped round the six monumental volumes of Tout's great work — elucidate, describe, and re-create the realities of medieval government. There are good reasons for this: for one thing, interest was bound to concentrate on the more obvious and also more important issues — religion, warfare, foreign relations, economic and social development; when matters of government attracted attention they tended to be seen in the "constitutional" guise — the rise of parliament, the powers of the crown, the place of the council. The humbler but quite fundamental matters of financial administration, the changes in the royal household, or the altered methods of the bureaucracy, have never been properly studied, and even the council has been the subject of "constitutional" rather than "institutional" investigation, so that we are better informed of its theoretical significance than of its practical history. This is not to say that research has not been made into this field, with most valuable results; in many ways, the most significant book on Tudor history for some time has been Professor J. E. Neale's approach to parliament from an institutional and administrative

From Geoffrey Rudolph Elton, *The Tudor Revolution in Government* (Cambridge, 1953), pp. 1–5, 7–8, 19–20, 67, 70–71, 415–417 and 424–427. Reprinted by permission of the Cambridge University Press.

point of view in *The Elizabethan House of Commons*. But there has been no co-ordination of results. Consequently the importance of the sixteenth century in the history of public administration — on which ultimately all constitutional progress must rest — has hardly been realized. . . .

The plain fact is that Henry VII ascended the throne of a medievally governed kingdom, while Elizabeth handed to her successor a country administered on modern lines. Much had gone, much been freshly invented, much profoundly changed, in the intervening century, even though a great deal had been simply preserved. We are familiar with the notion that the sixteenth century saw the creation of the modern sovereign state: the duality of state and church was destroyed by the victory of the state, the crown triumphed over its rivals, parliamentary statute triumphed over the abstract law of Christendom, and a self-contained national unit came to be, not the tacitly accepted necessity it had been for some time, but the consciously desired goal.

In the course of this transformation there was created a revised machinery of government whose principle was bureaucratic organization in the place of the personal control of the king, and national management rather than management of the king's estate. The reformed state was based on the rejection of the medieval conception of the kingdom as the king's estate, his private concern, properly administered by his private organization; it conceived its task to be national, its support and scope to be nation-wide, and its administrative needs, therefore, divorced from the king's household. It is one of the paradoxes of sixteenth-century history that a dynasty, which saw the personal power of the monarchy at its height and the importance of court life greater than ever, could also transcend the purely personal view of the royal duty and treat England and the nation as the true basis of the state. The personal impetus was needed to overcome past particularism; England was not able to do without the

visible embodiment of her nationhood until she had first passed through a condition where that visible embodiment was more obvious than the national foundation beneath. It will not do, however, to regard the Tudor state as a purely personal monarchy; the fact which underlay the well-known fellow-feeling of the Tudors and their people was that in reality the monarchy represented the nation — the nation called the tune. No amount of Tudor temper and bluster could disguise that fact. The most powerful dynasty ever to sit on England's throne was powerful only as long as it did not go outside the limits laid down by a nation at last fully conscious of its nationhood. The Tudor state was a national monarchy to a degree new in England, and while the apparent emphasis lay on the monarchy the real stress was already on its national character.

This is the meaning of the saying that the sixteenth century saw the making of the national state, and in that profound change administrative reform was bound to play its part. There had been bureaucratic organization on a national scale for centuries before, but the decisive and ultimate factor in medieval administration was the direct action of king and household. By the end of the sixteenth century the outlines of a purely national system had been drawn and largely filled in, and the subject of this study is the decade when the new principles were first consistently applied. It will be shown that, down to 1529, medieval government — household government in the broad sense — continued at work. The changes after 1530 in all sections of administration — finance, the secretariats, the king's council, the king's household — will then be discussed to show that new principles were indeed at work and profound reforms undertaken. This is a study of government at the centre only: local government, a vast subject in itself, needs separate treatment, though it has in any case been less neglected than have the institutions at the centre.

One of the outstanding differences between the medieval and modern periods lies in their attitude to individuals; in the modern age it is usually possible to discover and ascribe personal responsibility. Individuals assert themselves where anonymity had been the rule. Whether or not this had anything to do with the humanist revival of ancient ideas on such matters and with the Renaissance worship of the individual, it is a fact which is also, once again, reflected in the records. The state papers are personal material in a way that nothing medieval is; it has been said that they "make history possible in a fuller measure than ever before" by tearing aside "the veil which separates us from character and personality in the Middle Ages." In the 1530's, the state papers are largely what remain of the private archives of Henry VIII's second great minister, Thomas Cromwell. There are other papers, but their bulk does not compare with the products of Crowell's private office. There is a danger in this: it may be that Cromwell appears to dominate his age so much because his papers have survived. The accident of preservation ought not to be ignored, but it must not be overstressed. Even a casual glance shows that the scope of Cromwell's influence, the extent of his activity and power, and the attitude to him of others made him a special case: he was outstanding; and the record, though it may occasionally fail to preserve the activities and minds of others, cannot really be suspected of serious distortion when it sets the stamp of Cromwell on nearly everything done in these ten years, in the great issues of state and church as well as in the details of daily government.

* * *

A more realistic view of Cromwell can thus be obtained from a study of his work in government, but that is, after all, a by-product of the present purpose. Cromwell matters only in so far as one meets him at every turn in the story of administrative reform. If, as we hope to do, we can show the persistence of medieval methods down to 1529 and the subsequent modernization

of government, we shall have done something to restore to the sixteenth century, and in particular to the age of the Reformation, its old character as a time of real change. More and more the Tudor century is coming to be regarded as merely an extension of the middle ages, and this is a serious error. There is, let it be admitted, much danger in too easy a use of such terms as medieval and modern, and since they will have to be used much a word of explanation is due. Naturally many very typically medieval facts and opinions persisted into very recent days, even as many facts and opinions once thought of as typically modern have been traced back into the high middle ages. Naturally, too, any rigid division of past life into chronological periods can only lead to disaster. But he would be a bold man, and a bad historian, who would deny the existence of periods — even of moments in time — when things underwent changes so profound that only the word "revolution" can adequately describe them and only a firm date can place them. Such a period, such a moment in time, came in England when Henry VIII accepted Cromwell's advice to consolidate the territory he governed under the exclusive sovereignty of the king in parliament. An attitude to the state that can only be called medieval was at that moment replaced by one that can only be called modern. It will serve little purpose to quarrel over words: let these two terms be used as convenient summaries of inescapable historical facts. When this modern state in all its self-conscious independence had taken the place of the medieval state in which king, parliament, and even the nation occupied a much less ascertained place, not everything that had gone before was destroyed — not even most of it; but lack of true sovereignty was at the heart of the earlier dispensation, and the supremacy of the king in parliament was at the heart of the new. Where it mattered most a change had occurred which entitles us to speak of a revolution from the medieval to the modern state.

Methods of government reflect the constitution of the state they serve. Medieval household methods served the medieval state; modern national methods served the modern nation state. In that sense the terms are permissible in a discussion of administrative history. No one will doubt that the government of the fourteenth century was fundamentally different from that of the seventeenth. This difference lay in the abolition of the half-formal household methods characteristic of the middle ages, and in the adoption of the bureaucratic national methods characteristic of modern times; so much is common ground. That this change, this abolition and adoption, was inaugurated in the ten years between 1530 and 1540 shall now be shown.

*   *   *

The period from the battle of Barnet (1471) to the death of Henry VII (1509) marks the recovery and renewed consolidation of medieval kingship. The so-called New Monarchy of the Tudors is, as is well known, on the point of joining other traditional categories of historical writing in the lumber-room; 1485 may soon be a date of as little significance as 1760 has been since Professor Namier's[1] researches. More and more it is coming to be held that Henry VII did little that was not already started, or at least foreshadowed, by his Yorkist predecessors. What is not perhaps sufficiently realized is that by all standards of judgement this period of reconstruction after the civil wars had considerably more affinity with the past than with the future. Because strong rule was the most obvious characteristic of the Tudor century, the foundations of that rule have been taken to be the foundations of a new system of government, but the superficial symptoms have distracted attention from the underlying realities. Not only was kingship a very different thing after the Reformation and not before, but the means and methods — and, in a way,

even the objects — of government changed greatly after 1529. Especially as regards the administrative machinery, the whole period cannot be understood unless the characteristic of medieval government, namely household action, is kept in mind. Where we find administration in and through the household, there we have medieval government; where there are plentiful signs of emancipation from the household, however mingled they may be with survivals from the past, we may justly suspect the beginnings of a new attitude to government which for want of a better word we call modern. By this definition, which alone gives point to any classification of fifteenth- and sixteenth-century government, Edward IV, Richard III, and Henry VII were thoroughly medieval (as the following pages will show), though none the less strong and effective rulers. Medieval government, as Edward I proved conclusively, could be quite as efficient as anything that came after it, and Henry VII in particular was to make the point again and with even greater emphasis. There is thus little purpose in attempting to disentangle the originality of Tudor from Yorkist monarch, or in allotting responsibility. The record is much fuller for Henry VII, his dynasty survived, and his work was done more thoroughly and skilfully, for which reasons his reign matters more in the history of administration; but it is more important to trace the history of the various institutions throughout these forty years than to make an artificial division at the year 1485.

*   *   *

The reign of Henry VIII falls naturally into three major and two minor divisions: Wolsey's supremacy, Cromwell's rule, and the last seven years on the one hand, with the first three years and the interlude between Wolsey and Cromwell on the other. Every one of these periods has a character of its own; there is remarkably little uniformity about this thirty-eight years' reign of one king. Lack of colour and precise outline are typical of the two short periods,

[1] The late British historian who effected a "revolution" in the study of the Reign of George III. [Editor's note]

more obviously so of the second (1529–32) when great problems agitated the state and very manifestly were brought no nearer solution. Power abroad, the search for glory, energetic but uninspired administration at home, and financial weakness mark Wolsey's rule; revolutionary stresses, the grim execution of a detailed plan, efficient government, and financial skill stand out in Cromwell's time; vacillation, lack of direction, uncertainty in conception and action make Henry's last years a period of frequent failure and few achievements. To some extent, of course, these differences were due to altering circumstances, but the undisputable fact that such problems as arose were tackled in a strikingly different fashion at different times cannot be so explained. Each section of the reign differed from the rest in a manner which can only rationally derive from changes in the men who directed affairs. The king was always there, and though no doubt his character and even his abilities changed with advancing age, there is no development along any lines, however complicated, which would make it possible to see in these periods no more than the history of one man's life. The differences lay in the men he employed. This fact in itself goes a long way to substantiate the view that Henry was not, despite his overpowering personality and his ultimate control, the maker of his own policy; of course he alone could turn it into his own, but he did not invent it and relied on others for the mind that must inform action.

* * *

This is important. The government of England was at one time in the hands of Wolsey, lord cardinal and last medieval chancellor, at another in that of the "new man" Thomas Cromwell, layman and principal secretary, at a third in that of an immature and faction-ridden board. If we wish to understand the history of administration at this time we must understand something of the men who administered. Wolsey, eager to sit in state as a judge and to manipulate the strings of European diplomacy, contented himself with administering the country as he found it. Household finance, the traditional seals, a household itself insufficiently organized for its departmental duties, a council on the verge of turning into a court but unable to act as a board of government and hamper the minister, these were the weapons that he employed. Cromwell, on the other hand, was to show himself less easily satisfied, and he attacked the "medievalism" of English administrative institutions — the household core — in every particular, not of course sweeping the board and creating an entirely fresh set, but yet changing everything profoundly. Wolsey had looked after the administration because he wanted control and freedom to put his ideas into practice in the courts and in foreign policy; Cromwell, engaged in refashioning the very basis of the state, found it necessary to remodel its government. It therefore becomes advisable to see what kind of mind and attitude he brought to the business of government. With Thomas Cromwell, a modern type of English statesman took up the reins of power: the lay businessman and bureaucrat of genius whose sober dress has neither the flash of steel nor the cardinal's scarlet. Government had always been a professional business for the rank and file; now the man at the top was to be a professional and specialist too.

* * *

It will be well to review the conclusions already arrived at. It has been shown that between 1530 and 1542 . . . "household" methods and instruments were replaced by national bureaucratic methods and instruments. The household, driven from the work of administration in which for centuries it had acted as a mainspring and reserve, became a department of state concerned with specialized tasks about the king's person; finance fell to national institutions rather than to the personal servants of the king and those household offices which administered it before 1530; the secretary of state and the privy council stepped out of the household on to the national stage. Every reorganization that took place was in the direction of greater definition, of specialization, of bureaucratic order.

It would, of course, be wrong either to see no signs of such changes before 1530 or to believe that the work was all done by the end of that momentous decade. Yet the rapidity and volume of change, the clearly deliberate application of one principle to all the different sections of the central government, and the pronounced success obtained in applying that principle, justify one in seeing in those years a veritable administrative revolution. Its unity is further demonstrated and indeed caused by the personality which appears in every aspect of it. Thomas Cromwell, whose own career displayed the bureaucrat, was behind this deliberate and profound reforming activity. . . .

Whether the new administration was more efficient than the old is not the question here, but brief attention must be given to that point. Undoubtedly Cromwell and his assistants and successors believed it to be so, or they would not have laboured to make it. Undoubtedly, too, the theory of a national bureaucracy was more efficient than that of a household administration, since it depended less on the vigour displayed by the sovereign and was less bound up with his life. Continuity and the division of labour are the hallmarks of bureaucracy; they were as marked in the medieval exchequer and chancery as they are in any modern government department. But while the household remained the ultimate source of action, individual qualities and behaviour counted for more than the traditions of a department; to that extent the end of household administration was bound to assure greater reliability and efficiency. However, traditions take their time to grow, and Tudor government continued to depend on personality; indeed, government always depends on personality, as we can see to this day. There are only degrees in such matters: Henry VII's death jeopar-

dized his whole system of government, making necessary statutory and semi-bureaucratic organizations; Cromwell's fall only reduced the thoroughness, honesty, and efficiency of the system he had built up. The failure of medieval government in the Wars of the Roses compelled Edward IV and Henry VII to construct anew the agencies of government, even though they had example and precedent to guide them. The failure of Tudor government between 1540 and 1558 was redeemed by Elizabeth's council without major administrative reforms and merely by putting fresh energy and drive into the existing institutions. The reforms of the 1530's, the bureaucratization of government, succeeded in obtaining that continuity which marks modern government and prevents real anarchy even in days of civil war. In this most general aspect of efficiency the reforms did their work.

*   *   *

True administrative revolutions are in any case rare. Administration can never really stand still because it has to cope with changing conditions and the desires of new men at the top, but for that reason it usually develops sufficiently by slow degrees not to require rebuilding on new principles. It is only when the state itself is being refashioned fundamentally that revolutions take place in the methods of government. The Anglo-Norman creation of a centralized feudal state governed by the king in his household was one such revolution. It produced a system which endured until a new kind of polity arose. Even though offices of state might leave the household, even though all offices and even the household itself achieved a high degree of bureaucratization, the true driving force of government continued to be with the king in person and the men who immediately surrounded him. The restoration of good government by the Yorkists, Henry VII, and Wolsey, employing as they did the old methods of an elastic household system, proved that point. But the reforms of the

1530's did more than improve details of old practice. They cast off the central principle of centuries and introduced a new one. When an administration relying on the household was replaced by one based exclusively on bureaucratic departments and officers of state, a revolution took place in government. The principle then adopted was not in turn discarded until the much greater administrative revolution of the nineteenth century, which not only destroyed survivals of the medieval system allowed to continue a meaningless existence for some 300 years, but also created an administration based on departments responsible to parliament — an administration in which the crown for the first time ceased to hold the ultimate control. Medieval government was government by the king in person and through his immediate entourage. Early modern government was independent of the household, bureaucratically organized in national departments, but responsible to the crown. In present-day government, the bureaucratic departments have ceased to be responsible to the crown and have instead become responsible to the house of commons. It is important to note that these changes are most accurately reflected in what must be the basis of any administrative structure, the civil service itself. The medieval household system was served by men recruited from church and household; the middle period used clients of ministers, trained in their service and promoted by and through them; this second method of supply lasted until it was replaced by the modern civil service with its examinations. Clearer indication of the essential unity of these three periods, the many structural and methodical changes notwithstanding, could hardly be asked for.

There have been, then, only three administrative revolutions, though many more changes and reforms, in English history. As might be expected, they were the work of dynamic governments and of ages when the state itself was being made anew. Indeed, they were only one aspect of profounder revolutions affecting the nature of the society which they served. The Anglo-Norman system was devised to fit the royalist-feudal state, the state ruled by kings who were the heads of the feudal pyramid and the personal source of all government. The reforms of the nineteenth century produced an administration suitable for a parliamentary democracy, and the beginning of real administrative reform coincided significantly with the laying of the foundations for that state — the extension of the franchise and the introduction of the secret ballot. In its time, the Tudor revolution in government also coincided with changes in the structure of society and of politics. It accompanied, resulted from, and in a manner assisted in the creation of the monarchic nation state which prevailed in the sixteenth, seventeenth, and eighteenth centuries. Talk of a "new monarchy" in the sixteenth century has become a little unfashionable of late, while historians of thought associate the beginning of "modern times" with the scientific revolution of the seventeenth century. These views are assuredly a healthy and timely reaction against the old-fashioned division which, for instance, ignored the many things in Tudor England that were essentially medieval. But in some ways the reaction has gone too far; as regards political and social structure, the sixteenth century produced something quite new in England — the self-contained sovereign state in which no power on earth could challenge the supremacy of statute made by the crown in parliament. It will not do to dethrone the Reformation.

The fact has perhaps been obscured by the tendency to look upon the age of the Tudors as one homogeneous period to which the Yorkists ought to be added as prototypes and forerunners. Any view which would mark a really significant change in either 1471 or 1485 is indeed bound to fail. But if we admit that "the Tudors" were not simply a rather static lot established in position by Henry VII and thereafter content to copy his ways, if we endeavour to trace the real lines of change and development in a century whose dynamics have been neglected because it seemed stable in comparison with those that came before and after it — if we do this, we are inexorably forced to see quite astonishingly revolutionary changes in the 1530's. Any attempt to play down the effect of Henry VIII's political Reformation because it was not based on noticeable changes in mental atmosphere (itself a dubious enough thing) puts a very laggard cart before a steeplechaser. In England at least, more often than not, political events precede mental reorientation; events are commonly the result of physical forces and personalities, and many a thinker has limped along after the party to offer his quota of ideas in explanation and justification. It is enough if one man knows what he is about — and Thomas Cromwell, at least, knew that. The establishment of the royal supremacy over the Church, the expulsion of the pope, and the assertion of the unlimited sovereignty of statute destroyed the foundations of medieval polity and society and put something new in their place. Thomas More knew well why he opposed the voice of Christendom to an act of parliament, and Thomas Cromwell knew equally well what his assertion of the omni-competence of parliament meant. They both knew that they were witnessing a revolution. The general intellectual and spiritual effects of the revolution came later — as effects, not causes; but that does not make it any less of a revolution. This is not to deny that symptomatic indications can be traced back even over a hundred years, nor that further changes were necessary later. It is to assert, however, that in the years between the fall of Wolsey and the fall of Cromwell the changes are crowded together so thickly and so deliberately that only the term 'revolution' can describe what happened. In this revolution, in this making of a new kind of state productive of a new kind of society, the administrative reforms which have here been discussed played their part. It is against this background of controlled upheaval that they must be seen and understood.

THE BURGUNDIAN STATE

HENRI PIRENNE

The late Henri Pirenne was born in Verviers, Belgium, in 1862. For many years he served as Professor of Medieval History at the University of Ghent. Many of his chief works have been translated into English, making the great historian as well known on this side of the Atlantic as he came to be in Europe. His seven volume *History of Belgium* is merely one of his many works, but it represented the full impact of his interests in economic and social history and the revolutionary effect his studies had on Belgian history. Among his other important works the following stand out: *Belgian Democracy: Its Early History; Medieval Cities; Mohammed and Charlemagne; Economic and Social History of Medieval Europe.* The essay here reprinted was first presented as an address to the International Congress of Historical Sciences at Berlin, August 10, 1908.

I N the Europe of the fifteenth and sixteenth centuries, the state created in the Netherlands by the four dukes of Burgundy who succeeded one another from Philip the Bold (1384–1404) to Charles the Bold (1467–1477), and perfected later by Charles V., occupied a unique position, and presented special characteristics which differentiated it so completely from the other political organisms of the time, that it merits more attention from the historian than it has heretofore been accorded. The study both of its formation and of its governing institutions is, in fact, of a nature to throw new light upon the policy of princes at the beginning of modern times: upon the obstacles which this policy had to combat, the circumstances which favored it, and in short, its connection with the social and economic life of that epoch.

But, to begin with, what is meant by the expression, Burgundian state? It is a modern term, and did not make its appearance before the end of the nineteenth century. It was invented to provide an exact designation for the political union in which, between the end of the fourteenth century and the middle of the sixteenth, the seventeen provinces of the Netherlands were joined under the authority of a single princely house. Although for a long time this house possessed the duchy and county of Burgundy as well, these two territories formed no part of the state which it built up, the state we are undertaking to describe. The union between them was simply a personal one, and indeed, the Burgundian state of the North never had anything in common with the two Burgundies; it possessed its own life, entirely independent of theirs, and the institutions by which it was governed did not extend their action beyond its frontiers.

Although the name Burgundian state is modern, it is not arbitrary, but is based on historic fact and on tradition. The chroniclers and historians of the fifteenth and sixteenth centuries regularly give the name Burgundians to the inhabitants of Belgo-Netherland provinces. The briquet of Burgundy was at the same epoch the national emblem of these lands, where it is still to

From Henri Pirenne, "The Formation and Constitution of the Burgundian State (Fifteenth and Sixteenth Centuries)," *American Historical Review*, XIV (1909), pp. 477–502. Reprinted by permission of the *American Historical Review*.

be seen carved on the fronts of their town halls and on the keystones of their churches. Circle of Burgundy is the name given under Maximilian and under Charles the Fifth to the circle of the Empire which embraced these lands. In the early part of the sixteenth century, it is true, the humanists gave up the old appellation and substituted that of *Belgica* or Belgium, which was supplied to them by antiquity, and which, reappearing after centuries, designates the kingdom of Belgium to-day. Nevertheless, even in the seventeenth century, curious traces of the early state of affairs are to be found. It will be sufficient to call to mind here that at the end of the Spanish régime the vessels of the Catholic Netherlands (the Belgium of to-day) still bore on their flags the arms of the house of Burgundy.

The name, indeed, is merely a detail. The essential thing is to prove the long duration of this Burgundian state, established at the dawn of modern times between France and Germany, and represented on the map of Europe to-day by the kingdoms of Belgium and Holland. From the fifteenth century until the great upheaval produced by the French conquest at the end of the eighteenth, Burgundian institutions remained at the basis of the institutions of these two countries whose political destinies were so different, and it can be said with absolute truth that both of them, the Republic of the United Provinces and the Catholic Netherlands, retained to the end the clearly defined marks of their common Burgundian origin.

In spite of appearances, then, and notwithstanding the great transformations which it underwent, first at the end of the sixteenth century, through the separation of the Calvinist provinces of the north from the Catholic provinces of the south, and later in the course of the seventeenth century through the conquests of Louis XIV. in Artois, Flanders and Hainaut, the Burgundian state had a very long existence. This length of life may at first sight appear remarkable, for it would seem that the

characteristics which made it a thing unique in Europe, denied to it all the conditions indispensable to the maintenance of a political organism.

It must first be made clear, that although it belonged to the group of territorial states (*Territorialstaaten*) formed at the end of the Middle Ages, it differed from them in a very noteworthy manner. Like those states, it was the work of a princely house, and not of a monarchy, and, again like them, it consisted of an agglomeration of lands originally independent of one another. But while the other territorial states were built up of districts subject to the same suzerainty, it united regions dependent on Germany (Brabant, Hainaut, Holland, Zeeland, Luxemburg, etc.) with regions dependent on France (Artois, Flanders). It included within its frontiers a fragment of each of the two great states between which it lay. Its princes, until the reign of Charles V., were at the same time vassals of the emperors and vassals of the Valois. In short, the Burgundian state appears to us as essentially a frontier state, or, to speak more exactly, as a state made up of the frontier provinces of two kingdoms. The Scheldt, the most important of its commercial routes, separated *Francia Occidentalis* from *Francia Orientalis,* from the time of the Treaty of Verdun (843).

Of a hybrid nature even from this first point of view, the Burgundian state was still more so if we consider the peoples who dwelt in it. It was crossed not only by a political, but also by a linguistic frontier. Lacking unity of feudal dependence, it lacked, in a manner still more striking, national unity. It united a group of Romanic with a group of Germanic population. Walloons occupied all the southern portions — Namur, Hainaut, Artois, Gallic Flanders and southern Brabant; while people of Netherland speech, of Frankish or Frisian origin, dwelt in the northern provinces. A frontier state between two kingdoms, it was still more a frontier state between two tongues. By a singular coincidence, it constituted at the same time the point of con-

tact between the two great states of Western Europe, France and Germany, and the
two great peoples that have formed European civilization, the Germanic and the
Romanic.

Finally, in addition to these two peculiarities we must mention a third. For the
Burgundian state had no more geographic
than it had political or linguistic unity. Except in the southeast, where it was protected by the hills of the Ardennes, it was
open on all sides. Outlined on the great
plain of northern Europe, it presented no
natural obstacles, either on the side of Germany or on that of France. Of the three
rivers which crossed it, the Rhine, the
Meuse and the Scheldt, not one has its
source on Burgundian soil.

Thus, from whatever side it is regarded,
this state at first sight appears to have been
the work of arbitrary will, and of chance.
It seems nothing more than a confused assemblage of heterogeneous territories and
of people still more heterogeneous; a sort
of defiance that grasping and ambitious
princes, favored by circumstances, hurled
in the face of nature and of history. And
in fact, in the fifteenth century, Charles
VII. and Louis XI. in France, and the Emperor Sigismund in Germany, regarded it
as something illegal and monstrous, the
hateful result of an abominable usurpation.
In our days a large number of historians
have passed a similar judgment upon it.
The French are unanimous in considering
it a work of usurpation and violence accomplished by traitorous princes who endeavored to ruin the house of Valois from
which they sprang by raising against it a
rival power. In the Netherlands themselves, there is no lack of writers who, taking into account solely the resistance raised
by provincial particularism against the
dukes of Burgundy, see in the latter nothing more than grasping and brutal tyrants,
trampling underfoot the national liberties,
and owing their success to violence alone.

It is not difficult to demonstrate that
these opinions, inspired by national considerations or by an abstract liberalism

which fails to take into account the conditions of existence in the society of the end
of the Middle Ages, have no correspondence to historical fact. Far from having suddenly interrupted the course of destiny in
the Netherlands, and from owing its birth
merely to the caprice of bold adventurers,
the Burgundian state appeared as the cli-
max of a long historical evolution. It was
the result of the co-operation of a number
of political, social and economic forces, the
action of which begins to be perceptible in
the early Middle Ages, in those frontier
territories which it brought together. In
spite of appearances, its constitution,
though at first sight strange, is perfectly
natural. The special characteristics which
it exhibits have their sources, in fact, in all
the earlier history of the Netherlands. Undoubtedly a combination of favorable circumstances, or the chance, if such it may
be called, which at a given moment ex-
tinguished dynasties, threw open successions, and caused the outbreak of military
and diplomatic conflicts, contributed largely
to the success of the work achieved by the
dukes of Burgundy. But is it not the same
with all human events, and is not the important thing in this case to distinguish,
beneath the chance multiplicity of changing circumstances, the profound and permanent tendency, of which these circumstances have done no more than to hasten
the final result? [1]

*　　*　　*

The facility with which the results just
enumerated [2] were attained proves to what
extent they were prepared by history. If it
can truly be said that the territorial principalities did not of themselves seek the
Burgundian rule, at least it is clear that

[1] Here follows an extended treatment of the
events from the Treaty of Verdun (843) to the
reign of the great Burgundian dukes, intended to
justify Pirenne's view of the continuity and in-
tegrity of the history of the Netherlands. [Editor's
note]
[2] The unification of the provinces under the early
dukes of Burgundy. Completed by 1469. [Editor's
note]

they accepted it without serious resistance. . . .

Charles the Bold (1467-1477) completed and at the same time endangered the work of his father.[3] He completed it in seeking to extend his power over Guelders and Friesland, the annexation of which was to make of the Zuyder Zee a Burgundian lake. He endangered it on the other hand by the violence of his ambition, which, after having rendered all his subjects discontented, led him finally to the catastrophe of Nancy. There is nothing astonishing in the speedy outbreak of an almost unanimous reaction against the ducal rule. To be sure, the Burgundian provinces did not seek to separate from one another. The Great Privilege which they forced the heir of Charles the Bold to grant them in 1477 left their union unbroken. But by substituting for the power of the prince the power of the States General as the central authority of the state, they actually transformed the state into a confederation of autonomous territories. It was too evident that such a confederation would have been incapable of defending itself against such an adversary as Louis XI., whose policy immediately after Nancy aimed at the complete ruin of the house of Burgundy. And so, scarcely had Maximilian of Austria married Mary of Burgundy, when he is found devoting himself energetically to the restoration of the monarchical régime set up by his predecessors. From 1477 to 1493, he unceasingly resisted the territorial particularism openly sustained by France, which used against him the suspicions bred by the fact that he was a foreigner. But when with Philip the Fair (1493-1506) a national prince again mounted the throne, the lost ground was at once regained. The princely prerogatives were again in force, the great central institutions of the state were restored, and the States General, instead of persisting in their role of systematic opposition, henceforth co-operated with the sovereign. It is from this time forward that

the Burgundian rule became popular in the Netherlands, and sent down, so to speak, far-reaching roots. The great nobles, part of whom, under Maximilian, had taken sides against the prince, henceforth grouped themselves in a body about him, entered his councils and shared the highest offices of the state, the maintenance of which became the indispensable condition of the prestige which they enjoyed.

Philip the Fair had neither the time nor the disposition to pursue the projects of Charles the Bold and of Maximilian with regard to Guelders and Friesland. His reign, essentially pacific, went no further than the strengthening of the union between the old provinces, and saw the accomplishment of no conquests. But Charles V. was to complete the annexations which constituted, after 1543, the union of the seventeen provinces. He won Tournay from France in 1521, acquired Friesland in 1523, Overyssel and Utrecht in 1528, Groningen in 1536, and finally Guelders in 1543. Henceforth the Burgundian state was complete, and would receive no further aggrandizement.

The annexations of Charles V., quite unlike those brought about by Philip the Good, were all accomplished through war. The very energetic resistance which he had to overcome, and which was directed almost continually by the famous Duke Charles of Guelders, is not fully explained by the energetic intervention of Francis I. in the affairs of the Netherlands; to understand it, it is necessary to observe that the territories subjugated by the emperor had had, until the end of the fifteenth century, relations much less close with the old Burgundian provinces than those which had existed between the latter since the early Middle Ages. Guelders was more German than Netherlandish. As for Friesland and its dependencies, where dwelt a population as different in its speech as in its state of society from that of the country of Holland, it had struggled energetically from the twelfth century on against Holland's attempts at annexation. These attempts,

---

[3] Philip the Good, 1419-1467. [Editor's note]

which were finally successful under Charles V., proved that his conquests on the right bank of the Zuyder Zee and the Yssel were something more than the results of his ambition. To complete the building of the Netherlands and assure their security it was indispensable that they should surround on all sides the inland sea which indented them on the North and that they should absorb the duchy of Guelders, the point of which, advancing between the Meuse and the Waal, menaced at the same time Utrecht, Holland and Brabant. Charles V., in uniting them to the territories of the west, did no more, as we have seen above, than take his inspiration from a plan already completely outlined in the days of Charles the Bold.

This assemblage of seventeen provinces, then, half Romanic and half Germanic, which constituted the Burgundian state at its completion, was composed of two clearly distinct groups of territories. The first, lying in the basins of the Meuse and the Scheldt, and extending along the North Sea west of the Zuyder Zee, was formed during the reign of Philip the Good, by virtue of a long historic evolution and without encountering serious opposition, except in the territory of Liège, which reassumed its autonomy in 1477, and retained it until the end of the eighteenth century. The second, on the contrary, a necessary aggrandizement of the Burgundian possessions, was the result of a war of conquest, and was built up only by means of violent annexations. Still, once accomplished, these annexations were permanent. The advantages which they found in their union with the Burgundian state soon reconciled the populations which had struggled with the greatest energy against it. Thenceforth they no longer sought a separation. It is true that they always played a less active part than the old provinces in the political life of the state, and it was only toward the end of the sixteenth century that the constitution of the Republic of the United Provinces attached them indivisibly to the territories of the west.

At the same time that the Burgundian state was forming by the union of the territories of the Netherlands under the authority of a single dynasty, it finally severed the ties, already loosened, which still bound it to France and Germany. Already in 1435, by the peace of Arras, Philip the Good had secured from Charles VII. release from his position as vassal of the crown. On the other hand, he neglected to pay homage to the emperor for his Lotharingian lands, so that he appeared in reality as an independent monarch. The memory of the ancient kingdom of Lothaire certainly haunted his mind and the minds of his principal counsellors, and inspired him with the ambition to obtain in his turn a royal title. His son Charles was for an instant on the point of realizing this project, which would have set the final seal on the sovereignty of his house, and if after him there was no longer any serious question of raising the Netherlands to the rank of a kingdom, the political autonomy of the country none the less continued to gain strength. Under Charles V., the treaties of Madrid and Cambrai rendered perpetual the concession granted by Charles VII. to Philip the Good; the dependence on France was forever abolished in Artois and in Flanders; the Scheldt finally ceased to mark on the map a political frontier. It might seem, at first sight, that this advantage wrung by the Emperor from his adversary would be of profit to the Empire. This was not the case. Charles V. acted in the Netherlands as the successor of the dukes of Burgundy, and his power only served to make definitive their separation from Germany. The convention of Augsburg (1548) established them, under the name of Circle of Burgundy, as an independent state. If, in appearance, it recognized them still as an integral part of the Empire, in reality it detached them from it, for it accorded them, in all its essential features, the attributes of sovereignty. Thus ended, under the great-grandson of Charles the Bold, the long historic process whose principal phases we have endeavored to sketch. The double movement begun in the tenth century had come to an end; the provinces of the Netherlands were united, and between France and Germany a new political organism, the Burgundian state, had come forth into the light of day. The cord that bound together the seventeen provinces was securely tied; it broke at the end of the sixteenth century only, beneath the double pressure of the revolution against Spain and the religious revolution.

An agglomeration of principalities long independent of one another, the Burgundian state in the first place rested on the principle of personal union. Heir or conqueror of the different territories grouped under his authority, the duke did not reign over them by virtue of a power of superior sovereignty. Instead of bearing a single title, like a king, he was clothed with a multitude of special titles. He was at the same time duke of Brabant, count of Flanders, count of Hainaut, count of Holland, etc., etc. In passing beneath his sceptre each province had preserved its autonomy, its own constitution, its special institutions. Nothing is more heterogeneous, nothing more motley, at first sight, than this state made up of an amalgamation of small states, in each one of which the common prince ruled only as the successor of the former local prince. But this is only one aspect of the matter. From the personal union came necessarily a certain unity of government. The ideal of the dukes, like that of all the princes of the fifteenth century, was an ideal of monarchical centralization. They sought in a double manner to augment their influence at the expense of the local government and of the privileges which their various lands had obtained from their princes: first, by strengthening in each of them their own authority, and, second, by establishing, with a view to the general administration, and above the greater number of local governments, a certain number of central institutions. As it appeared at the time of Philip the Good, and as it remained under Charles V., at the time of its fullest development, the Burgundian state may be de-

fined as a plurality of autonomous territories forming a monarchical unity. A certain equilibrium was established by the force of things between the local liberties and the princely power. Had it been free to develop itself at will, the latter would have arrived at absolutism, but it had to take into account, from the very first, an opposition that it was unable to overcome. In each province it was obliged to respect the old constitution that it found in force, and its role was limited to making a place for the political centralization of the modern state, while treating medieval particularism with respect.

This political centralization was, moreover, favored by the social and economic changes which characterized the fifteenth century. It would be quite unjust to consider it as exclusively the work of the dynasty and inspired by its interests alone. In point of fact the princely interest was in many respects intimately allied with the general interest. The nascent capitalism and the economic individualism which was developing along with it, suffered from the privileges bequeathed by the Middle Ages to modern times, which hindered their free development. The municipal exclusiveness which opposed the power of the princes opposed also the development of commerce and the prosperity of the new ports. The state of subjection which the "good towns" imposed upon the open country hindered the introduction there of that capitalistic industry which was excluded from the urban communes by the rigid and superannuated rules of the trades. It is also plain that not only the country districts, but above all those new centres of economic activity such as Antwerp and the Holland cities, which were adapting themselves to the necessities imposed by the transformation of commerce and of navigation, were on the side of the princes and favored their policy. The monarchical innovations of the Burgundian period were opposed only by the privileged cities, resolved, like Bruges and Ghent, to preserve the monopolies and prerogatives that had had their day. Nothing is more characteristic on this point than the contrast between their attitude toward the prince and that of Antwerp. In the one case, economic exclusiveness went hand in hand with resistance to the progress of political centralization; in the other, the liberal and innovating spirit which inspired the townspeople of Antwerp made it the faithful ally of the ducal government. In short, the more a city had been privileged in the Middle Ages, the more it resisted the new régime, and therefore there is nothing astonishing in the fact that it is especially in Flanders, where the cities, during earlier centuries, had surpassed those of all other territories in freedom and influence, that the Burgundian policy found its most resolute adversaries. But the resistance of Flanders was inspired by the past and not by the present. Its great communes wore themselves out in heroic efforts to maintain a supremacy which was escaping them, and the loss of which they attributed to the government. They did not see — and it was not in their power to see — that along with the establishment of the Burgundian state and independent of it, there was going on in the Netherlands a displacement of the economic equilibrium, and that the commercial leadership was on the point of passing over to Antwerp.

The "innovations" introduced by the house of Burgundy into the provincial administration responded so well to the needs of the times, that before its arrival in the Netherlands their dawn is apparent. Already Count Louis de Male had established in Flanders, about 1369, a supreme tribunal, the *Audience,* which must be considered as the precursor of the *Council Chamber* instituted at Lille in 1386 by Philip the Bold. This council chamber, which was soon subdivided into a court of justice (the *Council of Flanders*) and a chamber of accounts, was the first modern administrative institution which the Netherlands had known. Similar institutions (the councils of Brabant, Holland, Guelders, Hainaut, Luxemburg; the chambers of accounts of Brussels and the Hague)

were introduced into the other provinces as they passed under Burgundian sway. Everywhere they had as results the substitution of educated magistrates for the communal aldermen (*échevins*), the restriction of superannuated privileges to the advantage of the "common good," the disappearance from the law of a multitude of archaic usages, the habituation of lawyers to the practice of appeal, the organization of the pursuit of criminals, etc. The chambers of accounts brought the administration of the finances to a regular accountability, exercised a permanent control over the receipts and expenses of all officials, and allowed alterations in the distribution of the taxes, rendering them more equitable. It is incontestable that the Burgundian administration merited the reputation for excellence that it enjoyed, and of this there is no need of other proof than the fact that it served as a model to Maximilian for the reforms he introduced into Austria.

As was natural, it is from France, where monarchical government was from the thirteenth century on so thoroughly developed, that the dukes borrowed a large part of their administrative system. But they were far from simply copying the institutions of that kingdom. On the contrary, they altered them considerably to adapt them to the special conditions of their country. During the early period, and this was one of the principal complaints uttered against them, they called in a goodly number of foreigners, Burgundians or Picards, to initiate into their new tasks the officials of the Netherlands. These assistants became less and less necessary in proportion as the new régime became established, and they had almost completely disappeared in the second half of the fifteenth century.

We have said above that the establishment of monarchical institutions did not go on without arousing protest and, at least in Flanders, even violent conflicts. In all the provinces, the cities had acquired a dominant influence, and the policy of centralization found itself consequently more or less openly at odds with the urban policy.

But, favored by the economic manifestations which were undermining the latter,
it triumphed everywhere without great ex-
ertions. The cities, though they retained a
large measure of autonomy, were obliged
to recognize the superior authority of the
state, submit to its control, and contribute
to the public expenses. If the rank and file
of the townspeople long remained faithful
to the old principle of municipal exclusiveness upon which rested the convenient industrial monopoly of the trades, the great
merchants and the capitalists, on the contrary, rallied very soon to a system of government in which the "common good"
took the place of privilege and in which
municipal freedom was restrained only for
the securing of a larger freedom. Moreover
the bureaucracy now furnished a crowd of
young patricians with a new and lucrative
career and, in the Burgundian state as in
all modern states, contributed powerfully
to rally the well-to-do classes to the monarchical régime which was the condition
of its maintenance.

Much less powerful than the cities, the
clergy and the nobility showed also less opposition to the "Burgundian innovations."
The excellent relations which the dukes
maintained with the papacy, moreover, prevented the former from struggling against
them with any chance of success. It re-
signed itself to the restriction of its jurisdiction and to the intervention of the prince
in the grant of ecclesiastical dignities, and
rapidly accustomed itself to a situation
where devotion to the dynasty was the best
path to success. As for the nobility, although it too had lost a considerable number of privileges and prerogatives, it was
compensated by lucrative and honorary offices which were thrown open to it at the
court, in the administration and in the
army, and the entire body was soon gathered about the prince.

Although so far-reaching, the reforms accomplished in the provinces left untouched
in all of them the ancient traditional constitutions. Everywhere the privileges accorded to their lands by the former princes

remained; everywhere the Estates retained
the right of voting the taxes and nowhere
was there any modification in the organization of these assemblies, which were the
essential organs of territorial autonomy.
The monarchical organization took possession of all the vast administrative and judicial domain left vacant by the rudimen-
tary organization of the Middle Ages; it
put an end to abuses, it modified and perfected existing institutions, but it did not
destroy them.

Besides the monarchical reforms accomplished in each province, the Burgundian
period also saw the rise of a system of
central institutions extending their action
throughout the Netherlands, and thereby
transforming them into that collective state
which we have endeavored to characterize
above. It is an entirely new political phenomenon. For where, before the end of the
fourteenth century, different lands had already been united under the rule of a
single prince, it is not observable that this
dynastic union brought about the slightest
community of government. The princes, it
is true, even when they reigned over several
countries, had but a single council; but this
council, made up of trusted advisers and
limited to a purely consultative part, did
not, properly speaking, constitute a governmental institution, and it seems scarcely
ever to have intervened except in questions
of foreign policy. Naturally the dukes of
Burgundy possessed a council of this sort
when they came to the Netherlands. This
council, made up of nobles, clerks and lawyers from their different domains, and even
of foreigners, was attached to the prince's
person and moved about with him, having
no fixed residence. But from the reign of
Philip the Good a decisive change took
place. Out of the original council developed two councils with special attributes:
one, the privy council, retained the consideration of political affairs; the other, the
Great Council, formed a high court of
justice with jurisdiction over the entire
Burgundian state. The latter, under
Charles the Bold, was definitely settled at

Mechlin under the name of *Parlement*; a name which it lost under Philip the Fair, to reassume and retain until the end of the eighteenth century that of Great Council. As for the political council, a new specialization of its functions divided it, under Charles V., into three separate councils residing at Brussels: the council of state (political affairs), the privy council (controversial and administrative affairs), and the council of finance. These were called collateral councils because they acted in conjunction with the prince, or his representative, the lieutenant-governor. Henceforth, above the local governments of the provinces, there existed a general government which, acting in the same manner upon each of them, united them in a common action, and made them participate, in some fashion, in the same political life. And as we have shown above for the provinces, the central government at the end of the fifteenth century took on a national character, and excluded the foreigners that were numerous at the outset. Brussels, which was its seat, and in which after 1531 the sovereign's representative resided, became the capital of the Netherlands.

But, and this is one of the most interesting of its peculiarities, the central government included not merely institutions charged with developing and applying the authority of the prince. The creation of the States General by Philip the Good in 1463 gave the representatives of the country a part in it. This great assembly, made up of delegates from all the provincial Estates, not only gave the prince an opportunity to deliberate with his subjects as a whole; but it also provided the most potent of the means of unification which had brought together the seventeen Burgundian provinces. Finally, just as the monarchical institutions did not suppress the territorial institutions which were anterior to them, so the States General did not absorb the individual Estates. On the contrary, it was with the latter that the final decision rested. Without their assent, the deputies of the States General could conclude nothing.

Thus particularism remained as powerful beside the central organ of national representation as beside the institutions of monarchical power, and from whatever side it is examined, the Burgundian state always presented the same spectacle of modern unification above and medieval diversity below.

But while diversity did not increase, unification realized constant progress in the course of the fifteenth and sixteenth centuries. The creation of the Order of the Golden Fleece in 1430 attached to the person of the prince all the great nobility of the Netherlands, and thus put at his disposition, in the different territories, the enormous ascendancy which it enjoyed. On the other hand, the formation of a standing army (*bandes d'ordonnance*) under Charles the Bold enabled the dukes to take into their pay almost all of the lesser nobility, who, in fighting under their standard, were soon imbued with a lively sentiment of Burgundian loyalty. In conclusion, political measures, such as the Convention of Augsburg (1548) and the Pragmatic Sanction (1549), the former by placing all the provinces in the same position with regard to the Empire, the latter by unifying the right of succession in such a manner as to secure in each province the perpetual maintenance of the dynasty, constituted new reasons for cohesion among all parts of the Netherlands.

But while the state was thus strengthening itself within, its position with regard to the dynasty suddenly changed. Philip the Fair, who, after the troubled regency of Maximilian of Austria, had been hailed with enthusiasm as the successor of the earlier dukes and the restorer of the house of Burgundy, became in 1504, at the death of his mother-in-law Isabella of Spain, the heir of the kingdom of Castile. It became straightway evident that in the near future the sovereign of the Netherlands was to have other interests than theirs to guard, and that it was to be expected that he would subordinate the peace and possibly the prosperity of the Belgian provinces to the world-politics into which he would be drawn. The premature death of Philip (1506) postponed the realization of these fears. But the young Charles V. succeeded to his father's rights, and therefore, to prepare as far as possible for what the future held in store, the endeavor was made, in spite of his grandfather Maximilian and his aunt Margaret of Austria, so to direct his education as to make of him a purely Burgundian prince. But the inevitable had to come to pass. Of how little weight were the Netherlands in the political combinations of a prince who reigned at the same time in the Empire and in Spain, and whose ambition had all Europe for its field! Although he accomplished, as we have seen, the territorial unification and the system of government of the seventeen provinces, in return he laid upon them expenses and wars entirely foreign to their interests. At the end of his reign Artois, Hainaut, Namur, Luxemburg, had been laid waste by French armies, and the unimpeachable credit of the Antwerp market, weakened by loans, was tottering. Nevertheless, the services rendered the country by Charles, the renown which dazzled the nobility fighting for him, the sympathy, at least apparent, that he showed his Burgundian subjects, together with the prudent conduct of the two regents, his aunt Margaret and later his sister Mary, to whom he had entrusted the government, neutralized until the end of his reign the sentiments of opposition which were gathering in the public mind. These sentiments broke out suddenly at the accession of Philip II., as soon as it was recognized that this prince was a thorough foreigner, antipathetic to the character of the country and hostile to its liberties, and that he clearly aimed at making the provinces Spanish. Ten years had not elapsed after the final departure of the king (1559) before the Netherlands were in open revolt. And this result, far from recalling the particularist uprising of 1477, proves the strength that the cohesion of the provinces had gained since that time. Directed by the principal lords of the council of state, unanimously sustained by the lesser nobility belonging to the bands of ordonnance and by the popular masses of each territory, it appears as a collective effort *viribus unitis;* as an insurrection of the Burgundian state, desiring to maintain its independence against the Spanish state. Indeed, it is more than this. During its progress, the Burgundian state became the nation, and it was in this period of heroic struggles that its people for the first time gave it the name *"communis patria."*

Unfortunately the unanimity of the resistance was not to last. With the complication of the political by the religious question, the national party divided itself into Protestants and Catholics. William of Orange did not succeed in preventing a scission that had become more and more inevitable. It finally came about during the last years of the sixteenth century. Of the two fragments of the Burgundian state, one, the republic of the United Provinces, was in the following century to attain to that unheard-of degree of prosperity which remains in the history of Europe an unparalleled phenomenon; the other, the Catholic Netherlands, drawn into the decadence of Spain, was to vegetate in obscurity under its foreign governments and serve as a battle-ground for the armies of Europe. Its sovereigns left it its old Burgundian institutions and respected its internal autonomy. But, deprived thenceforth of the direction of its destinies, tossed about at the mercy of all the political fluctuations in the midst of which Spain went under, it lost its own self-consciousness, and long lay benumbed in provincialism and routine, after having, at the beginning of the seventeenth century, given forth one final gleam.

CROWN AND ESTATES
IN THE LOW COUNTRIES

HELMUT GEORG KOENIGSBERGER

Professor Koenigsberger was born in Berlin in 1918. He was trained in England, however, at Gonville and Caius College, Cambridge. Since 1960 he has served as Professor of Modern History at Nottingham. His chief interest is in the history of representative and parliamentary institutions in France, the Low Countries and the dominions of Philip II. Among his most important studies are *The Government of Sicily under Philip II*, which broke new ground in the development of our understanding of the nature of monarchy in that area, as well as many articles on the development of resistance to Spain in the Low Countries.

PARLIAMENTS and representative assemblies, the basis of modern democratic institutions, have had an unbroken history in only two countries of Europe; yet, in the later middle ages, they played important parts in the political life of nearly every European country outside the Italian and Swiss city states. In some kingdoms, as in Sicily, they survived up to the eighteenth century as respectable guardians of ancient privileges without, however, seriously rivaling the powers of the monarchy. Elsewhere, they either disappeared altogether, like the States General of France, or they lost all real power and influence, like the Cortes of Castile or the *Landtag* of Prussia. Only the English Parliament, the States General of the Netherlands (and perhaps, though with some serious interruptions, the *Riksdag* of Sweden) established themselves permanently as equal, or superior, partners of the monarchy in the control of ultimate power in the state. Of these the States General of the Netherlands maintained itself only in the seven northern provinces of the Burgundian dominions; but there its

victory was so decisive that, at least formally, it displaced the monarchy altogether.

These events are well-known; they have generally been studied as aspects of the revolt of the Netherlands in the latter part of the sixteenth century. Not so well-known is the history of the States General before the great revolt. Although, from the time of Gachard, Belgian historians and archivists have made sporadic attempts to collect material for such a history, it has not yet been written. Yet this history is essential to the full understanding of later events; for the States General of the Netherlands played a most important rôle for more than a century before the days of Calvinism, the Water Beggars and William the Silent. Most of the claims put forward by the States General during the revolt against Philip II had precedents during the previous hundred years. Twice, in 1477 and in 1488, the States General became the instrument of revolutionary movements, claiming powers and performing actions which were traditionally reserved to the monarchy. If

From H. G. Koenigsberger, "The Estates General in the Netherlands before the Revolt," in *Studies Presented to the International Commission for the History of Representative and Parliamentary Institutions*, vol. VIII pp. 141–158. Reprinted by permission of the author and the publisher, E. Nauwelaerts, Louvain, Belgium.

its successes were short-lived, on these occasions, it remained a potential centre of opposition to the monarchy, an alternative focus of power in the state; and while its members might, for long years, remain almost unaware of this, it was never entirely forgotten — least of all by the monarchy. . . .

The States General of the Burgundian provinces *de par deça*, later to be called the Netherlands, had no definite date of birth. Each of the provinces which the house of Burgundy added successively to its possessions had its own provincial estates with its own well-established powers and traditions. In 1430, Philip the Good summoned the estates of Brabant, Flanders and Holland to a joint assembly at Malines in order to discuss the high price of English wool, a question in which all three provinces were vitally interested. Following repeated requests by the towns of Brabant, Flanders, Holland and Zealand, the duke summoned another joint assembly of the towns of these provinces at Ghent, in 1434, to discuss English competition in the cloth industry. There followed further assemblies to which varying groups of provinces were summoned to deal with problems of trade, the reform of the coinage or other matters which concerned more than one of the provinces under the duke's rule. In the history of these assemblies there is no evidence that Philip the Good deliberately set out to create a States General as a new institution designed to give greater unity to his dominions. The joint assemblies were summoned because it suited all parties concerned to discuss specific common problems in this way, and these problems were nearly all questions of economic policy. At no time during his reign did Philip ask these joint assemblies for financial help — he did, of course, ask for *aides,* or *beden,* from the separate provincial assemblies — and not until 1464 did an important political question appear on the agenda. Only thirteen years later, at the death of Charles the Bold in 1477, the States General acted not only as a recognised and self-conscious in-

stitution but as the claimant to the ultimate control of political authority in the Burgundian dominions.

For much of the rest of the fifteenth century, however, the States General preserved many of the characteristics of a largely functional and *ad hoc* institution. Right through the sixteenth century it remained primarily an assembly of the delegates of provincial estates, reflecting the varying composition and interests of these latter bodies and especially their particularism. Thus Flanders, the richest and most powerful of the provinces, was generally represented in its provincial estates by its «four members», the cities of Ghent, Bruges, Ypres and the *Franc* of Bruges, the important country district of western Flanders where political control was largely in the hands of the lower nobility. In Holland the voice of the «six large towns», Dordrecht, Amsterdam, Haarlem, Leiden, Delft and Gouda, was equally overwhelming. The nobles had only one vote against their six, and the clergy had long since ceased to attend the Holland assemblies altogether. In Brabant, Artois and Hainaut all three estates were represented but, especially in matters of taxation, the consent of the towns was most important for the government, and most difficult to obtain; for the towns, unlike the nobility, could not shift the burden of taxation onto other shoulders. In Hainaut this meant, in practice, the towns of Mons and Valenciennes and in Brabant always the four «capitals», Brussels, Louvain, Antwerp and Bois-le-Duc.

The representatives who attended the meetings of the provincial estates were, in fact, little more than delegates of the towns who sent them to the assemblies, who paid their salaries and expenses and whose instructions they had strictly to follow. The nobles and prelates could either attend in person or also send representatives. The powers of the representatives at the meetings of the States General were similarly limited: in consequence no clear-cut distinction can be made between the history of the States General and the history of the provincial estates. Many of the problems which had faced the dukes in their dealings with the estates of their separate provinces therefore reappeared immediately in the States General. Successive governments tried hard to induce the provincial estates to grant their representatives to the States General full powers so that agreements on taxation and other matters might be reached quickly. But the estates clung stubbornly to the system of limiting their delegates' powers. The delegates themselves — burgomasters, aldermen or pensionaries (i.e., salaried law officers) of the towns — saw no cause to diminish the powers of their town councils. Moreover, this very limitation could prove very useful in defensive tactics against the financial demands of the crown which could often be delayed for weeks and months by the obligation to refer back to the provincial estates and, beyond them, to the towns. In the assembly of May 1476, Charles the Bold's chancellor, Hugonet, driven to exasperation by the stone-walling tactics of the delegates, finally asked sarcastically whether their authority was also limited in the number of times they might drink during their journey. . . .

The meetings of the States General therefore had the appearance of a congress of delegates from quasi-autonomous powers, rather than that of an institution representing the country as a whole. During the fifteenth century it was never definitely established which particular provinces should attend, and membership varied a great deal. Gradually, however, conventions for membership hardened. When, in 1534, Charles the Fifth's government proposed a defensive union and a standing army for the provinces, the States General objected that these proposals were unacceptable while some of the provinces who would have to be part of the union never attended the assemblies. The provinces which were now regularly summoned were Holland, Zealand, Flanders, Brabant, Malines, Namur, Lille-Douai-Orchies, Artois, Tour-

nai-Tournaisis and Hainaut with Valenciennes.

The two problems, that of the membership of the States General and that of the powers of the delegates, were both aspects of a more fundamental problem: the divergence of interests between ruler and subject. It was the aim of successive Burgundian and Habsburg rulers of the Netherlands to weld their dominions together into a greater political unity and to provide them with more efficient and powerful government. Against these centralising policies prelates, nobles, towns and provinces set their traditional privileges and autonomies. Heavy and steadily increasing demands for money by the government, on the one hand, and unwillingness of the subject to pay, on the other hand, were the key to this relationship. At the same time, neither side pursued its policy consistently; all were fundamentally interested in carrying on the government of the country as peacefully and as harmoniously as possible. The right of the «natural prince» to govern was never seriously questioned until traditional loyalties had become frayed by years of bitter civil and religious war, in the second half of the sixteenth century. Thus, contrary to all reason and experience, the citizens of Ghent preserved a blind and pathetic trust in the emperor when they rebelled against his governor-general in 1537–40. On the other side, the rulers never made a frontal attack on the liberties of the country. It was a matter of pride or, at least, an effective propaganda point, that the Netherlanders lived in greater freedom than the subjects of the king of France, and that their prince did not arbitrarily impose taxes on them. Despite Charles the Fifth's occasional reluctance to summon the States General, no serious attempt was made to dispense with it altogether until the reign of Philip II and even then no less an autocrat than the duke of Alva tried to have his proposed taxes approved by the assembly.

Nevertheless, the relationship between crown and estates was ultimately a question of power. The claims of both sides had finally to be resolved by the victory of one or the other and, until that happened — as it happened sooner or later everywhere in Europe — there was bound to be a shifting balance of power. This became apparent at the very beginning of the career of the States General in the dispute over its claim to assemble independently of a ducal summons. . . .

This dispute, however, was bound to recur. If the estates could establish the right of assembly without ducal summons, then their independent authority was assured. Nevertheless, they were rarely willing to quarrel with the government over this point unless they had other reasons for quarrel as well. . . .

Much less clear-cut was the attitude of both States General and government towards the problem of joint debates and discussion between the various delegations. The provinces and estates represented by these delegations were deeply jealous of their autonomy and, in general, insisted on reference back, rather than on discussion with other delegations. In practice, however, common discussion between the representatives of at least two or three provinces was unavoidable if agreement was to be reached at all, especially on the government's demands for *aides*. The deputies of the smaller provinces were often instructed to follow the lead of Flanders and Brabant and to discuss a common policy with the deputies of the provinces. The attitude of the government was also ambivalent. Common discussions meant more rapid decisions on the government's proposals, and this was convenient. Moreover, if an important delegation had been persuaded to give a favourable vote, that would set a good example to the others. On the other hand, the resistance of Flanders or Brabant to a grant might equally well persuade others to resist too. This was one of Mary of Hungary's constant worries. . . .

But at the beginning of Philip the Second's reign, when the political system of the Netherlands was beginning to break down, government policy began to oscillate vio-

lently between the two approaches to the problem of common discussions. The strain of the seemingly unending French wars, economic depression and famine prices, the quarrels between the estates and the higher nobility over the latters' claim to exemption from payment of the *aides* — all these combined to make the subject more unwilling than ever to grant the king's financial demands. Finally, the government despaired of coming to terms with either the States General or with the estates of Brabant and, in September 1556, sent high government officials to the Brabant towns to negotiate with each separately for an *aide*. But this attempt at by-passing the estates altogether met with no success and, a year later, the policy was completely reversed. In November 1557, the deputies appeared at the States General, for once with full powers and the government decided to allow them to meet in joint session to discuss the financial position. The result was indeed a compromise on the *aide* demanded, but it was coupled with a long list of grievances and petitions on matters of high policy. Thereafter Granvelle, and probably Philip II as well, became convinced that the States General could no longer be trusted.

It was over taxation that the interests of crown and States General were most clearly opposed. Throughout this period it was generally accepted that the prince had a right to expect financial help for the defence of the country. When, however, wars continued for years on end, when defence, turning into agression, demanded ever greater sacrifices, the loyal suubjects not only resisted the demands for money but began to question the conduct of the government's foreign policy: when Charles the Bold's wars which had demanded such heavy sacrifices ended in the catastrophe of Morat and the duke's death at Nancy, the Netherlanders rose in revolt and the States General claimed for itself the control of foreign policy. But neither by its tradition nor its constitution was the States General fitted to carry on the tasks of government;

its control over foreign policy broke down within a few months. The conflict with the government, however, continued. . . .

Not until 1576 did the States General make similarly determined forays into a sphere of government normally reserved to the prince; but the fundamental problems persisted through the sixteenth century. During the reign of Charles V there was only one open revolt, that of Ghent, 1537 to 1540, and that was more in the nature of a tax-paying strike than of revolutions such as those of 1477 or 1488. But the interminable, destructive and apparently senseless wars with Guelders, and the increasingly expensive and dangerous wars with France, produced an intermittent, but gradually swelling, rumble of dissatisfaction with the emperor's foreign policy. Twice, in 1512 and in 1522, Margaret of Austria feared the imminent outbreak of rebellion. Complaints continued that the Netherlands were made to conquer Italy for the emperor and Denmark for the Count Palatine. The joint session of the States General, in November 1557, was particularly outspoken on these points.

More effective than their intervention in foreign policy were the attempts of the provincial estates and, later, of the States General in its turn, to control the collection and expenditure of the taxes they voted. Since, as everywhere else in Europe, there was at that time a chronic shortage of efficient and reasonably honest civil servants, successive governments were not in principle opposed to a development which relieved them of the onerous and unpopular task of collecting taxes. More and more the estates insisted on such control before they would grant any *aides* at all. In 1513, Margaret herself suggested that the States General should appoint its own commissioners to supervise the government's collection and expenditure of the taxes they should vote. The offer was rejected at that time; for the States General insisted on peace with Guelders. But in the 1520's and 1530's, the estates of Flanders, Brabant and Holland all built up their own machinery of con-trol. In 1558, the States General took the first step towards creating a unified financial institution under its own control for the whole of the Netherlands by appointing the Antwerp banker, Antoon van Straelen, as superintendent of taxes for all the provinces.

While the monarchy was not entirely averse to such developments it was distinctly hostile to the growing habit of the estates of demanding redress of grievances and the acceptance of petitions before they would grant *aides*. In vain, provincial governors and governors-general tried to reverse this procedure: the estates knew that without such insistence their power was broken, and they remained adamant. Mary of Hungary even said that the estates preferred the emperor to be poor so that they should be more powerful, «for, through their privileges, they wanted to be masters and not servants».

Even when the patrician deputies themselves were willing to meet the government's financial demands, fear of their constituents at home often prevented them from doing so. In Brabant and, before 1540, in Flanders, the petty bourgeoisie of gilds and craftsmen were represented in the town councils and had to approve all financial decisions. They were perfectly capable of holding up agreements of the whole States General, as did the gilds of Brussels and Louvain in the early years of the reign of Philip II. Charles V pursued a consistent policy of excluding the more democratic elements from the government of the Netherland towns; but even where the lower classes were thus excluded there was the constant fear of riots and open revolts. The great towns of Flanders, in particular, were the centres of popular revolutionary movements. Since these movements often started as revolts against heavy taxation, and since those aldermen and burgomasters who were held to be too accommodating to the government's demands were liable to lose their heads, these popular movements tended to strengthen the estates in their resistance to the crown and were generally responsible for the more extreme parliamentary claims. This happened in 1477 when popular movements broke out all over the Netherlands. It happened again in Flanders during the rebellions against Maximilian, in 1485 and 1488.

Nevertheless, the patrician oligarchies usually remained in firm control of the towns and, in consequence, also of the States General. Their interests were local and sectional; the privileges they defended against encroachments by the crown were equally local and sectional — often diametrically opposed to the interests of other towns and provinces. Such was the case, for instance, when Holland claimed to export grain freely while there was famine in the rest of the Netherlands. In the absence of a general cause for opposition, it was therefore most unlikely that the government would ever be faced by a general revolt of the States General, and, in fact, no such movement occurred during the whole long reign of Charles V. The States General remained a conservative force, capable of blocking important government policies disliked by the majority of provinces, such as the proposed union and standing army of 1534-35, but unable and unwilling to challenge the crown's control of government. Yet the political situation remained unstable and tended to deteriorate, especially after about 1530. The Brussels riots of 1532; the revolt of Ghent of 1537–40; the confederation of the abbots of the great Brabantine monastic houses, formed to resist the financial demands of the crown; the increasing friction between the estates of Holland and the governor, the count of Hoochstraten — all these were signs that Charles the Fifth's imperial policy was overstraining the resources of the Netherlands and the goodwill of his subjects.

During the first years of Philip the Second's reign, the States General became the mouthpiece for grievances which had now become general: excessive taxation and the presence of Spanish troops in the Low Countries. During the governor-generalship of Margaret of Parma, the king became convinced that, if summoned again, the States General would become the mouthpiece of the movement to moderate the placards against the heretics and the activities of the Netherlands inquisitors. Philip was undoubtedly correct in his estimate of the situation; yet it was not the States General which initiated or organised the revolt. The economic changes of the sixteenth century had upset the social equilibrium of important areas of the Netherlands and had thus created a revolutionary situation: among the artisans and wageearners of the industrial belt of WalloonFlanders Calvinist preachers found a fertile field for their propaganda, and they were similarly successful among the middle and lower classes, alike in the thriving port of Antwerp and in decaying old textile towns like Ghent and Leiden. The country-nobility saw their incomes dwindle with rising prices and their local influence curtailed by the extension of the activities of the central government: many hundreds joined Louis of Nassau's and Brederode's Compromise. Calvinism, working on social and economic discontent, created forces and organisations which transcended provincial boundaries. These forces saw in the States General a convenient weapon and called aloud for its summons — and this at the very moment when the king's policy had antagonised some of the most powerful members of the high nobility. Thus the stage was set for the series of revolts which began in 1566. The subsequent collapse of the crown's authority left the States General in the centre of the political stage as the only legitimate political authority. But internal divergencies of interest and aim, and insufficient control over those external forces which had created the revolutionary movements, prevented the States General from keeping the Netherlands united.

FRANCIS I, HENRY II, AND THE ESTATES

J. RUSSELL MAJOR

Professor Major was born in 1921. After attending to his undergraduate education, he interrupted his training for a term of military service spanning the years 1942–1945. He then took a Ph.D. at Princeton. Since 1949 he has served in the Department of History at Emory University. In the years since 1949 Professor Major has spent an appreciable part of his time in French archival collections, focusing on the representative institutions of Renaissance France, time well spent, if we can judge from the series of books and articles he has written. Included among his chief works are the striking study of the representatives who actually participated in the Estates General sessions of the 15th and early 16th century, as well as studies of the *Estates General of 1560* and *Representative Institutions in Renaissance France.*

THE MONARCHY OF FRANCIS I

"Francis I and Henry II were as powerful as any other kings of France; it was at the beginning of the sixteenth century that the absolute monarchy triumphed." So wrote Georges Pagès, one of the leading authorities on French constitutional history. There is certainly evidence to support his position. The assemblies of the three estates of the kingdom virtually ceased, the towns were not convoked after 1517, the notables were summoned less often to give advice, the estates were not asked to ratify treaties after 1544, and there was a growth of absolutist political theory. Furthermore, the Concordat of 1516 gave the crown effective control over appointments to important church positions, the seizure of the bulk of the Bourbon inheritance in central France removed the greatest of the French nobles from the scene, and the reorganization of the administration of finance further strengthened the crown. Yet with all these changes, the popular, consultative nature of the monarchy continued unmodified for the first third of the period and was only mildly altered thereafter.

Francis I had "neither the strength of mind nor the steadfast will to apply himself to a systematic transformation of society and institutions." He was preoccupied with foreign affairs and war. The few changes he instituted arose largely from the need for money for foreign enterprises. He sincerely believed the Bourbon inheritance to be his; he was so far from trying to destroy Charles of Bourbon, the greatest of his vassals, that he named him Constable of France and Governor of Languedoc and Milan soon after he came to the throne. Indeed, Francis I loved his nobility as no other French king had. On them he heaped honors, pensions, and court positions. It was the nobility who profited most from the Concordat, for they received the finest ecclesiastical benefices. It was in part to have them near him that he built huge châteaux. They were his companions in arms and in the chase. The young king was knighted by the bravest of their number and asked no better than to be called "the first gentleman of France."

Nothing could be more erroneous than to accept the statements of several Venetian ambassadors that Francis I could tax his subjects as much as he pleased. It is true that wars and extravagance made an increase in the taille necessary. The revenue from this tax stood at 2,400,000 livres in 1517 and was gradually increased to 4,600,000 by 1543, a figure no higher than that reached under Louis XI in 1481. During the intervening sixty years, prices had nearly doubled, and the capacity of the French people to pay had grown considerably. But the ability of Francis I to tax, like that of his predecessors, was dependent on public opinion. There was an ill-defined, but nonetheless definite point beyond which he could not go without provoking revolt. When he reached that point, he had to turn to expedients, and this he did early in his reign. Substantial parts of the domain were sold, as were the crown jewels, and even some of the treasures of the churches; offices were created and made venal, wages of officials were taxed, loans were demanded, and a system of public credit was instituted. Such measures, though sometimes arbitrary, were not those of an absolute monarch who could tax at will. Only the favored nobility escaped almost intact from the financial manipulations of the king, and they were the principal beneficiaries of his largess.

THE DECLINE OF THE CONSULTATIVE
ASSEMBLIES

The first few years of the reign of Francis I saw the most important administrative changes that were made between his succession to the throne in 1515 and the death of his son in 1559. During this period there was a large amount of consultation. On September 10, 1516, Francis ordered the towns to send deputies to Paris on October 15 to give advice on what should be done about the perennial currency problem. The deputies met several times with Chancellor Duprat in the *hôtel de ville*, but according to Jean Barrillon, the secretary of that official, no solution was reached and the deputies returned to their homes having accomplished nothing. Whether the deputies really contributed anything or not, cannot be said, but on November 27 an ordonnance was issued upon the advice of the council, the various financial courts, and "some delegates of several of our good towns of our kingdom" which set the value on various coins.

Francis instructed the towns to send deputies to Paris on March 15, 1517, to give advice on how the kingdom could be enriched. Seventeen towns and the provincial estates of Provence and Brittany responded to his summons. This time the government took steps to ensure orderly proceedings, a precaution one suspects that had been neglected in the October assembly. The letters of convocation stipulated that one or two economic experts be chosen, and efforts, for the most part unsuccessful, were made to get the towns to comply with this regulation. When Troyes elected an advocate, the *procureur* of the town, and a seigneur, the chancellor asked the municipality to send instead two merchants, whom he named, because they knew more about the matters to be discussed than anyone else. A similar fate may have befallen Dijon, for the municipal council reduced the original delegation from seven to two, but then in a show of independence elected the town scribe and a councilor to accompany them. Nevertheless, in spite of the royal directives, less than half the towns limited themselves to one or two deputies and most of those chosen were municipal officials, not merchants. Indeed, many deputies were nobles, a few being of the sword, and clergymen were in the delegations from Rouen, Tours, and Bayonne.

The first meeting of the assembly was held on March 21 at the court of Parlement. The judges had been carrying on a battle against the Concordat that the king had just concluded with the papacy, and it had been decided to explain the new policy to the deputies and the members of the sovereign court at the same time. The crown hoped to rally the support of the towns as a counterweight to the opposition that was being offered by the judiciary and some ecclesiastics.

Chancellor Duprat initiated this policy.

Before Francis I, several princes, the Parlement, and the deputies, he began by pointing to the domestic problems and foreign enemies the king faced on his succession to the throne. He glorified the great victory that the young ruler had won at Marignano. He argued that the enemies of France had persuaded the pope to abolish the Pragmatic Sanction and assume control over appointments to benefices in the French church. To halt these evils, the king had concluded the Concordat which, it is true, made some changes in the matter of ecclesiastical elections, but nevertheless preserved the essential features of the Pragmatic Sanction and made possible peace with the papacy.

The restoration of peace, the chancellor continued, had freed the king to turn his attention to domestic affairs. The principal persons of the various courts of the realm had been assembled to evaluate old ordonnances and recommend new ones, expenses had been reduced, and an assembly of the deputies of the towns had met to advise on the preparation of a decree establishing the value of the currency. The present meeting was designed to secure the enrichment of the people. Duprat's ideas on how this enrichment should be accomplished were purely mercantilistic. He spoke of the fertility of France which produced all that was needed and made imports unnecessary. He admitted that there were several gates through which money was brought into the kingdom, but added that there were several through which it left. The latter were, for the most part, unwarranted and ought to be closed to allow money to be drawn from but not returned to neighboring states. To secure this enviable situation, the king desired that certain proposals be placed before the assembly.

These proposals were not submitted to the deputies of the towns on that day, but rather were read to them on March 25 in a meeting held in the *hôtel de ville*. They consisted of nine articles designed to prohibit the importation of foreign goods, ensure the use of French ships in foreign trade, set the value of French currency, establish a single system of weights and measures, limit the use of luxury goods, and the like.

After the articles had been read, they were discussed for two days without any agreement being reached. Instead of giving advice, many deputies wanted to submit cahiers bearing on the needs of their individual towns. At length, the government decided to break up the assembly. The deputies were sent home with copies of the articles to be debated in assemblies of the larger and wiser part of the inhabitants of their towns. The conclusions were to be transmitted to the king to be utilized in the preparation of an ordonnance for the enrichment of the kingdom. Steps were also taken to communicate the articles to the smaller, unrepresented towns in the bailiwick of Dijon and possibly elsewhere to secure their opinions.

Jean Barrillon reports that when the letters containing the advice of the towns reached the capital, they were placed unopened in a big leather sack and spoken of no more. Perhaps the secretary of the chancellor exaggerated a little in his disgust at the work of the assembly, but no ordonnance emerged based on its deliberations and no further calls were made on assemblies of the towns for advice during the reign. Barrillon leaves no doubt as to the reasons for his unhappiness over the outcome of the meeting. The government had presented a mercantilistic program designed to stop the flow of money out of France by halting the importation of goods, and the deputies had opposed this move in favor of a policy which permitted greater freedom in trade. This attitude, to Barrillon, indicated that the deputies preferred their individual profit to the general good. Another thing that irritated him was the tendency of some of the deputies to insist that their individual complaints be satisfied before they would pay attention to the proposals of the king. On this last point, we suspect, there was justice in Barrillon's position. When asked to make recommendations on what should be done to enrich the kingdom, the deputies from Troyes could only suggest that the holding of the *Grand jours* of Champagne and Brie in their town be confirmed and that they be given permission to have another fair. The problem of fortifications seems to have dominated the ideas of Bayonne. To the bureaucratic Barrillon, the towns were too motivated by self-interest to make it worth-while to consult them. It was for officials like himself, who presumably were above local prejudice and had only the general good in their hearts, to prepare ordonnances for the government of the kingdom. He gave no indication that he feared representative assemblies. Rather he opposed them because he thought they were useless. One suspects that his attitude was shared by many.

There were no further assemblies of the towns during the reign of Francis I, but it would be virtually impossible to prepare a list of all the nonrepresentative assemblies. Ordonnances were usually made and issued on the advice of great nobles and the regular members of the council, though vague references to "other notable persons" were not infrequent. In addition, specialists were consulted now and then. For example, some captains took part in the preparation of the army regulations issued in June, 1526, and financial officials helped prepare an ordonnance forbidding the export of gold in December, 1529. Records have usually survived only for assemblies held in conjunction with the Parlement of Paris, where the clerk of the court carefully noted who attended. Often these assemblies took the form of a *lit de justice*. Present would be the king, prelates, great nobles, bailiffs, members of the Parlement, and others in widely varying numbers. In his *Recueil de rangs des grands de France,* the clerk, Jean Du Tillet, listed more than twelve meetings during the reigns of Francis I and Henry II as examples, but on the whole there was a marked decline in the use of large consultative assemblies after the first few decades of the period.

THE ESTATES AND TREATIES

There were many interesting meetings concerned with foreign affairs and treaties. They began with a series of assemblies on the Concordat made with the pope in 1516. This treaty was to be ratified by the French church and the various courts of Parlement within six months, but it was unpopular because it gave the king effective control over important ecclesiastical appointments and made probable the revival of the *annates* abolished by the Pragmatic Sanction. With a degree of caution, Francis approached the problem of ratification. Twice he had it approved by his council, with several ecclesiastics and members of the sovereign courts being present. Then on February 5, 1517, he appeared before the Parlement of Paris accompanied by several great nobles, important ecclesiastics, canons of Notre Dame, and representatives of the University of Paris to ask that the Concordat be registered by Parlement and ratified by the clergy. After some speeches, the members of Parlement and the clergy separated to discuss their replies. When the two groups reassembled, the Cardinal of Boissy reported in the name of the ecclesiastics that the entire French church was interested in the Concordat and that it could be ratified only by a general assembly of the clergy. The king was angered, for he had hoped that this rump assembly would serve as the means of satisfying his agreement with the pope to get the consent of the clergy. The reply of the Parlement was noncommittal.

On March 21 the matter was placed before a joint meeting of the deputies of the towns and the members of Parlement in the hope of rallying public opinion to the side of the new arrangement. On May 29 the king renewed his demands on the Parlement for ratification, but after much debate the court refused. For nearly a year the quarrel continued, until, at length, the Parlement abandoned its stand before the threat of the king to reduce its jurisdiction by creating a new court at Orléans. Immediately after his victory, Francis took steps to secure ratification by the provincial courts. The University of Paris continued to resist for a short time, but eventually it too was silenced, and the Concordat of 1516 became one of the principal decrees which regulated the French church. The consultative traditions of the monarchy had been violated, not so much by the enforced registration of the Parlement — for here the king was clearly within his constitutional rights — but by the failure to get the consent of all the French clergy as had been agreed with the pope. Francis' action was undoubtedly caused by the belief that the Gallican Church could not be persuaded to accept the proposed changes. The affair is of interest because it shows that in the ratification of treaties, the Parlement and the other institutions consulted were no mere rubber stamps, even though they were eventually persuaded to accede to the royal desires. . . .

During this period there was some talk of convoking the Estates General. The matter came up in the Parlement . . . but it was decided not to press for a meeting. . . . Louise of Savoy was definitely opposed to the idea because the three estates had in times past claimed the right to name the council during a regency. It seemed to her that those who sought a meeting of the Estates General could only desire her removal, and on October 8 she reproached a member of the Parlement saying that several councilors of that court wanted to see the estates of the kingdom assembled to diminish her authority. This charge the Parlement steadfastly denied.

The unfavorable attitude of Louise of Savoy towards convoking the Estates General should not be interpreted as a general policy of the monarchy; it only meant that she did not feel the moment was opportune. A decade earlier, when Francis had named her regent during his first Italian campaign, he had issued two orders defining her powers. In the first, dated July 15, 1515, he had included a vague statement that she could do whatever was necessary for the good of the kingdom. This phrase he clarified that same day in the second order giving her authority to make ordonnances and "to assemble . . . the people of the estates of our kingdom. . . ." When he again named her as regent on August 12, 1523, he gave her the power to summon the members of the sovereign courts, other crown officials "and likewise the mayors, échevins, councilors, bourgeois, men, and inhabitants of the towns of our kingdom, and our other subjects . . . in order to have their council and advice. . . ." Later in the same document and with almost the same phraseology as in 1515, the queen mother was given authority to convoke "the people of the estates of our kingdom. . . ." Would Francis have authorized his mother to hold meetings of the estates if he had feared these assemblies? Would not the easiest way to protect her from such demands have been specifically to deny her this right? Yet in 1515 in order that there be no uncertainty in his first declaration of her powers, he had issued a second statement specifically giving her the authority to consult the estates. No less a person than Chancellor Duprat advocated assembling the three estates when news of the disaster at Pavia reached the court. Later, Francis was made so desperate by the demands of the emperor that he issued a letter from captivity ordering that his eldest son be crowned king and that his mother act as his regent. To inform the people of these changes, he further directed that the three estates be assembled. . . .

The negotiations for Francis' release offer another interesting example of the role of the people in foreign affairs. In March, 1525, Charles V demanded the return of Burgundian territories taken by France in 1482, the surrender of French claims in Italy, and other concessions. He insisted that these terms be ratified and approved by the French estates, the Parlement of Paris, four provincial Parlements, the various *Chambres des comptes,* and the members of the council. Francis replied in April. He balked especially at the surrender of Burgundy on the grounds that it was allied to the crown of France, and stated that ratification by the estates, the Parlements, and the *Chambre des comptes* was impossible unless the terms of the treaty were modified. Whether Francis' refusal to secure the ratification of the treaty in the desired manner was based on his belief that the estates would not consent to the dismemberment of the kingdom as he said, or whether his attitude resulted from a desire to use the estates as an excuse not to make major concessions, cannot be determined; but he was not motivated by fear of consulting the assemblies because he made counter proposals that included winning the approval of the Parlement of Paris and the estates of France.

By December, 1525, Francis was desperate enough to move a long way toward meeting the territorial demands of the emperor and expressed his willingness to see the treaty ratified by the courts of Parlement and the three estates of France. The final terms of the Treaty of Madrid of January, 1526, provided for freeing the king in return for the surrender of two of his sons and twelve great nobles as hostages. These hostages were to be returned as soon as Burgundy had been delivered to Spain; the Estates General had promised the perpetual observance of the treaty; and the various courts of Parlement and the *Chambre des comptes* of Paris had registered it.[1]

*   *   *

The next great treaty of the Habsburg-Valois Wars was signed at Crépy in September, 1544. As a Cambrai the terms called for ratification and approval by the provincial estates and for registration by all the Parlements and the *Chambre des comptes* as Paris. In spite of similarity in the phraseology concerning the method of rati-

---

[1] Here follows a long discussion of the use of consultative assemblies, which declined in frequency enormously between 1525–1544. [Editor's note]

fication in the two treaties, it seems probable that this time approval was given by the provincial estates as stipulated, rather than by the estates of the bailiwicks and seneschalsies. The agreement was ratified by the estates of Languedoc, Burgundy, Normandy, Picardy, and presumably other provinces.

The final treaty in the long wars between the two dynasties was signed at Cateau-Cambrésis in April, 1559. This time the approval of the provincial estates was not required, only that of the Parlements and the *Chambre des comptes* was retained. Did this omission mark the growth of absolutism and a decline in the popular, consultative nature of the Renaissance Monarchy? This is possible, but one suspects that estates were also dropped because European rulers had come to believe that their oaths to support and maintain treaties were useless. Time and again the estates had made these vows, sometimes even swearing to help the Habsburgs against their own king, but we do not know of a single instance of their doing anything when their king broke the treaty, as he invariably did. Philip II knew what his father had never learned, that a people can be as warlike and as dishonest as a king. It is true that registration by the Parlements and the *Chambre des comptes* had not prevented violation of treaties by French kings either, but registration was advisable for legal as well as diplomatic reasons and was therefore retained.

THE GROWTH OF THE THEORY OF ABSOLUTISM

The decline of the number of assemblies and the failure to use the estates to ratify treaties was paralleled by a growth of absolutism in political thought. The theorist par excellence of the earlier stages of the Renaissance Monarchy had been Claude de Seyssel. His *La Grand' Monarchie de France* was written to instruct Francis I, who had reigned only four years when it was first published. Following the general pattern of the medieval theory of kingship, he depicted the ruler as being limited by the religious life of the state, *la justice,* and *la police*. The religious check not only required the king to conform to the rules of the Catholic Church, but also bound him to adhere to the general principles of justice. *La justice* involved more specific limitations on the authority of the crown and empowered the courts to give redress when the king encroached on the rights of his subjects. *La police* included the fundamental laws governing the succession to the throne and the inalienability of the royal domain as well as the rights, privileges, and customs of the various social groups. The king, Seyssel admitted, could annul or change bad customs and laws, but one of his primary duties was to maintain those that were good. Taxes should be light, but for taxing he did not require popular consent. He also closely followed the practices of the early Renaissance Monarchs by insisting that rulers get advice before taking important action. In addition to the small, frequently consulted *Conseil Ordinaire* and *Conseil Secret* to handle ordinary affairs, he discussed the larger general councils which were of two types. The one, known as the *Grand Conseil*, consisted of the leading clergymen, nobles, great officers of the crown, and members of the sovereign courts. The other, which he referred to as the *Assemblée Casuelle,* included, in addition, the deputies of the principal cities and towns of the kingdom. It would be inconvenient, he thought, to summon either of the general councils too often, and he relegated to them only matters of great consequence to the whole kingdom: the question of war or peace, the preparation of laws and ordonnances concerning justice and administration, and the like.

However, during the two or three decades which preceded the outbreak of the Wars of Religion, a new group of jurists headed by Grassaille, Rebuffi, and Chasseneuz began to advocate a theory of kingship that permitted some expansion of royal power. The checks of religion, *la justice,* and fundamental law were maintained in a slightly altered form, but there was a marked tendency to give the king more authority to override customary law, and much less was said about the various types of consultative assemblies that Seyssel had treated in some detail, though, of course, the advisability of taking council was still insisted upon.

THE SURVIVAL OF THE RENAISSANCE MONARCHY

The Renaissance Monarchy was threatened, but one must not exaggerate the danger. The new developments in political theory had little immediate influence on the thinking of the average Frenchman. One strongly suspects that the jurist was read only by his fellow jurists. Neither nobles nor burghers were affected as their behavior in the Wars of Religion was to prove. Nor was the decline in the use of the various types of national consultative assemblies paralleled by a fundamental change in all the other popular aspects of the government. The two reigns actually saw the development of diocesan assemblies of the clergy and the occasional use of provincial and even national clerical assemblies. The cause of the innovation was the need for the clergy's consent to taxation. At first Francis asked the clergy for financial assistance about every third year, but between 1541 and 1558 royal demands were annual. The amounts involved were substantial. Henry II never asked for less than 4 décimes, or about 1,600,000 livres, except in 1550 when he contented himself with half that amount. Consent was most often given by diocese, a procedure that led this type of local assembly to flower at the very time the large consultative meetings became less frequent. Not until 1561 did the first estate get its assemblies organized on a national basis, but the idea had slowly developed during the preceding half century.

There was no comparable system of assemblies for the nobility during the period, because the kings were either unwilling or unable to get them to pay taxes. The only time they were assessed, and therefore assembled, was to free the royal hostages held by the emperor. For this purpose, as we have seen, both a national and many local assemblies of the nobility were held between 1527 and 1529.

The declining use of the assemblies of towns did not mean that the municipalities were cut off from the central government. Letters were frequently sent back and forth between officials at the capital and those in the towns. More significant was the constant flow of deputies from the towns to court. Hardly a year went by but that a municipal council had occasion to send someone to the king concerning the privileges of the town, to request that some restriction be removed, or to ask that a tax be reduced.

Amiens can be used as an example. On March 6, 1539, the *échevins* heard the report of the town clerk who had been to the king at Fontainebleau on various affairs. On May 8 another official was paid for a visit to the king to prevent the transportation of wheat. On June 3 an Italian inspected a gun emplacement between a tower and one of the gates of the town on order of the crown. An anticipated royal visit was discussed, and plans were made to help the royal harbingers when they came looking for lodging. On July 3 it was once more necessary to pay deputies who had been to Paris on the business of the municipality. On September 18, it was the king who summoned representatives from the town to him about some matter. On October 23 an *échevin* and a companion who had been to court made their report. Among the privileges they had won was the right to levy a sales tax in the town for ten years without assembling the people, a real triumph for the municipal oligarchy. On December 12 a deputy was dispatched to Paris to see about a case before the Parlement which concerned the town.

It made no difference whether Amiens sent deputies to assemblies with the other towns of France or the three estates of the kingdom. The representatives of Amiens were as likely to be heard by the king if they were dispatched when the *échevins* felt the need. More likely, indeed, for then they could get the undivided attention of the monarch. To suppose that only the three estates meeting together could get a reduction in taxes is to miscontrue the nature of the Renaissance Monarchy. Actually when a town petitioned a king — even Francis I — and asked with good cause that a tax be removed or diminished, it was more than likely to receive a favorable reply. After all, it cost the king far less to reduce the taxes on a single town than on his entire kingdom.

Another way in which the kings maintained contact with the townsmen, as well as their other subjects, was through travel. Rarely did one of the Valois stay more than a month or two in the same place. This itinerant life gave many of their subjects chances to see their king and perhaps to petition him. These wanderings gave the rulers personal knowledge of the condition of their kingdom and the problems of each locality, an advantage that the eighteenth century kings who shut themselves up at Versailles sadly lacked.

Then there were always the provincial assemblies. It is not necessary to prove that the three estates of Brittany, Normandy, Burgundy, Languedoc, Dauphiné, Provence, and some smaller outlying provinces met regularly during these years, that they kept their right to consent to taxation, often reducing the amount requested, and that they performed many other services useful to themselves and to their king. It is true that a few historians of the estates have professed to see the decline of these institutions during the period of the Renaissance Monarchy, but we can only agree with Henri Prentout that they have offered no real evidence to substantiate their conclusions.[2] Indeed, the period of the Italian Wars brought increased financial demands, and the provincial estates were summoned more often than before.

[2] Prentout was an historian of the generation before Major; his special interest was in provincial representative assemblies. [Editor's note]

One only criticizes Prentout for not going further. He failed to stress the development of the assemblies of the clergy and he failed to note the meetings composed primarily of the third estate. The thirteen towns of Basse-Auvergne met regularly to vote taxes during the sixteenth century. What happened between 1451, the date Antoine Thomas chose for the demise of the provincial estates, and the reign of Francis I, we can only guess, but the existence of the assemblies is beyond dispute. In Guyenne there was a representative institution composed primarily of the deputies of the third estate from eleven seneschalsies and numerous local assemblies as well. The early history of these estates is not known, but they were flourishing in 1561 and were still functioning in 1616. The conquest of Piedmont provides further evidence of how little the principles of the monarchy had changed, for Francis continued to summon its estates to vote taxes and to perform other duties.

In spite of the continued vigor of the provincial estates, the decline in the use of national consultative assemblies would in the long run have led to significant changes in the nature of the Renaissance Monarchy had not other factors intervened. Just as the divorce question and the Protestant Reformation brought about a revival in the use of the English Parliament under Henry VIII, so military defeat, financial exhaustion, and religious disunity led to the revival of the large assemblies in France. This revival began near the end of the reign of Henry II and offered the last great opportunity for the establishment of the Estates General prior to the Revolution.

THE GERMANIES:
PRINCES AND PARLIAMENTS

F. L. CARSTEN

F. L. Carsten has devoted his professional energies to the study of the origins of the German national state. His important works include a number of articles and books, among them his noteworthy study of *The Origins of Prussia*, an important specialized study on the impact of the Thirty Years' War; extensive archival research into the history of a number of the 'petty' German states and his justly famous *Princes and Parliaments in Germany*, which performs a major service, in that it deals with the roots of the Liberal tradition in the many Germanies of the so-called Age of Absolutism.

I N the course of the later Middle Ages Estates came into being in the large majority of the German principalities, whether lay or ecclesiastical. In the latter they were usually dominated by the cathedral chapter of the see in question if the principality was a bishopric, but the Imperial abbeys also had Estates of their own. In the lay principalities the clergy often formed the first Estate, but they did not

From F. L. Carsten, *Princes and Parliaments in Germany* (Oxford, 1959), pp. 423–434, 436–438 and 441–444. Reprinted by permission of the Clarendon Press.

everywhere attend the diets, for example, not in the duchies on the Lower Rhine. In many other principalities they disappeared as an Estate with the introduction of the Reformation. Some Protestant principalities, however, such as the duchy of Württemberg, retained a clerical Estate. In others, such as the landgraviate of Hesse or the electorate of Saxony, a substitute was found in granting representation to pious foundations, hospitals, schools, and universities, so that the pattern of three Estates was preserved. In other principalities only two Estates were left, and these also predominated elsewhere: the nobility and the towns. The nobility sometimes were divided into the higher and the lower nobility, the former comprising counts and lords, the latter the much more numerous knights and owners of noble estates, unless they were commoners. In most principalities all noblemen who fulfilled certain qualifications with regard to birth and property had the right to attend the diet; but in the duchy of Prussia, and later also in the landgraviate of Hesse-Cassel, the noblemen first met in primary assemblies to elect their deputies to the diet. In many parts of southern Germany, moreover — in Baden, Württemberg, the Palatinate, Bamberg, Trier, and in certain smaller principalities of Swabia and Franconia — the nobility in the early sixteenth century succeeded in gaining the status of Free Imperial Knights and thus disappeared from the diets, which henceforth were attended only by the clergy and the towns.

Usually all the towns, including small market-towns, were summoned to the diet. But on the lower Rhine this right came to be vested in a few "principal towns" only, and in the duchy of Prussia the one important town, Königsberg, remained separate from the small towns, exactly as did Rostock and Wismar in the duchy of Mecklenburg. As the more important towns rose to the rank of Free Imperial Cities, the small territorial towns could not rival the influence of the nobility which throughout remained the leading Estate. The excep-

tions were those principalities where the noblemen became Free Imperial Knights; but in the duchy of Cleves too the towns became more important than the nobility. Most of the territorial towns, however, were declining, either already in the fifteenth and sixteenth centuries or as a result of the Thirty Years War. Thus the nobility, in spite of its own economic difficulties, remained the leading class, socially as well as politically, throughout the Empire and in the whole of central and eastern Europe. A *bourgeoisie* in the French sense, a middle class in the English sense of the term, did not develop in these small towns before the nineteenth century: hence the unchallenged lead of the nobility at the courts, in the offices and appointments, in the armies and the Estates of the German principalities. Among all the territorial towns of Germany only one could claim to be a city of real importance before the nineteenth century, and that was Leipzig; but it did not influence the history of the Saxon Estates to any large extent, nor did it attempt to challenge the leading role of the nobility.

The peasants were only represented in the diet as an exception, above all in frontier areas close to Switzerland and the Netherlands: in Tyrol and Vorarlberg, both Habsburg possessions, in the nearby abbey of Kempten and the archbishopric of Salzburg, in the margraviate of Baden, in the counties of Frisia and of Mörs on the North Sea. In several of these principalities the nobility did not attend the diets. In others, such as Württemberg and the Palatinate, the circumstance that the peasants were theoretically represented was indicated by the fact that the urban deputies sat simultaneously for the towns and the *Ämter*, the country districts around the towns. In Cleves and Mark, as well as in the duchy of Prussia, representatives of the peasants participated in the local assemblies which preceded or followed the diets. There the deputies were elected, or rendered their accounts, the business of the diets was discussed and concluded, the taxes were repartitioned, and matters of local government considered.

Thus the number as well as the composition of the Estates varied greatly from territory to territory. If the original pattern was the same as in France and other continental countries and contained three Estates, and accordingly three separate houses, this pattern was modified to such an extent in practice that it is almost impossible to say what was the rule and what the exception. In most of the lay principalities the nobility, and next to them the towns, formed the backbone of the Estates, and this corresponded to the reality of the *ancien régime*. But it also proved a barrier to a progressive constitutional development when the social reality began to change, and the nobility began to lose its importance. The composition of the Württemberg Estates was exceptional, not because the nobility no longer was an Estate of the duchy — that was the same elsewhere in southwestern Germany — but because of the presence of Protestant prelates who sat together with the urban deputies, which gave to the Estates a unicameral character. This factor and the common social background of the two Estates gave to them a coherence and a unity which were absent elsewhere. The friction which generally prevailed between the nobility and the towns was an element of weakness, which could easily be used to play off one Estate against the other and might enable an ambitious prince to curtail the power of the Estates altogether.

Broadly speaking, Estates developed everywhere in Germany in the fourteenth and fifteenth centuries for two reasons. One was financial: the princes' revenues from lands, jurisdictions, tolls, mines, and other *regalia* shrank owing to wars, economic difficulties, and the declining value of money so that many lands and rights had to be pawned or sold. This, however, merely aggravated the problem, for it diminished the princes' own revenues further and further; and they were correspondingly less and less able "to live of their own."

Hence they had to seek the aid of their subjects and to reach an agreement with the nobility or the towns about the terms on which they would be willing to render such aid. A famous example of such an agreement concluded at a very early time was the treaty of 1283 between the margraves of Brandenburg and their vassals about the tax of the *Bede* or *precaria,* according to which the margraves sold the tax to their subjects against a fixed annual due from land and property, and promised that they would not ask them for another tax in future, unless in two definite and specified exceptional cases. Yet this was only a temporary solution, for in the course of time the new fixed due was also sold or paid off, and the princes were more than ever unable to meet their growing expenses and to pay their debts. In their own interest a more permanent arrangement was necessary. They could have continued to negotiate with individuals, with certain districts, or with certain groups, but they found it much more convenient to negotiate with "the country" as a whole; and this was the origin of the Estates as an institution, as a corporation representing the whole country. Soon they granted taxes to their prince, but only against certain concessions and on conditions which became the object of elaborate bargaining. Soon the diet became the only place where such taxes could legally be granted, or at least this was the case in the opinion of the Estates.

The other factor which created the Estates as an institution was the endless succession of internal conflicts, fratricidal wars, and partitions of territory between brothers and cousins of the ruling families which filled the fifteenth century in particular. In such conflicts and civil wars either side had to attempt to win the support of the "country" without which they were helpless. Frequently the Estates were called upon to act as arbiters, to carry through or to guarantee a treaty, a settlement, or a partition, or to provide the regency council which was to rule on behalf of an infant prince. The history of all the German principalities is full of examples of this kind. Thus the Estates acquired political influence and began to wield power. In Brandenburg their representatives were called upon in the fifteenth century to sit as judges in cases between the margraves and refractory towns which declined to pay taxes or to open their gates to the prince. In certain instances the Estates used their newly-won powers to impose a kind of tutelage on a weak ruler, or they deposed him if he broke previous undertakings and treaties. Naturally, the Estates were strongly opposed to partitions of the territory and to the continuation of internal strife, which they sought to prevent by the conclusion of "unions" among themselves, implicitly or explicitly directed at their warring princes. . . . The Estates were equally opposed to sales of parts of the territory or of princely domains. They thus indirectly worked for a strengthening of the principalities, and opposed the idea that the princes could treat their territories as if they were their private property and could sell lands at their pleasure.

There is little doubt that at the outset the princes found the advice of the Estates on foreign and domestic issues useful and the aid of "the country" indispensable on account of their increasing debts; while the Estates were naturally reluctant to enter any new commitments and burden themselves with new obligations. They did not want to become a part of the new state, but to maintain their autonomy and their privileges. The princes showed the same attitude towards the Empire, and the nobility of the south-west towards the principalities from which they succeeded in emancipating themselves, becoming Free Imperial Knights. It was to the advantage of the prince to have a working institution which would come to his aid in case of need, rather than to have to negotiate with individual groups. . . . The Estates did not come into being as a planned move by one side or the other, but they grew up because they fulfilled a useful purpose, exactly as

did the English Parliament. One must be very careful not to transfer the later clash of interests, the conflicts of the seventeenth and eighteenth centuries, into a period where no such conflicts existed. As the "King in Parliament" was more powerful than the king alone, so the ruler "with Estates" was stronger than he was without them; for they provided him with the means to develop the machinery of government and with the money which he so urgently needed.

Finance remained the main field of the activity of the Estates. From the point of view of the prince the main, and often the only, reason for summoning a diet was that he needed money. From the point of view of the Estates the diet provided an opportunity to raise their grievances and to make their grant dependent on the fulfilment of certain conditions. As the prince and his councillors were often incapable of managing the country's finances, and as his credit usually stood very low, the Estates of many principalities took over the prince's debts, partially or totally, with the intention of gradually paying them off, which was hardly ever possible. . . . Taxes could be levied only with the Estates' consent, and this principle became the cornerstone of their liberties and their whole position; but a strong prince would at times levy taxes by decree without consulting the diet.

Using their right of raising grievances the Estates often tried to influence their prince's foreign and domestic policies, to make the conclusion of alliances and the starting of military operations dependent on their consent, to subject the composition of the princely council to their supervision, to make the appointment of officials dependent on their being natives of the principality in question, and to gain the right of being consulted in all important affairs. They were successful in pressing these demands to a varying degree, and the rights thus obtained were incorporated in their privileges, which every new ruler on his accession had to swear to observe. But again a strong prince would not necessarily consider himself bound by such promises and would tend to conduct his policy without a reference to his Estates. In the sixteenth and seventeenth centuries, however, many Estates strongly influenced the policy of their prince, prevented arbitrary actions and petty tyranny and, by their cautiousness in granting supply, avoided many an adventure in the field of foreign policy. . . .

The Estates had no claim to participate in legislation other than money grants. But in practice draft laws and decrees were often submitted to them, whether they were concerned with codifications of the law or legal procedure, police matters, trade, the coinage, the order of succession, or the administration. Often they seized the initiative in such matters through the grievances which they raised. In one field they were most strongly interested, that of religion, in which every individual felt most intimately concerned. As the dissolution of the monasteries in many ways violated the established rights of the clergy and the nobility, the Estates considered that the new religious order and the use of the ecclesiastical revenues were matters best to be arranged by the diet. It is true that in most Protestant principalities the Reformation was introduced without any prior consultation with the Estates. Only in Brunswick was their consent obtained by the Duchess Elisabeth, acting on behalf of her minor son. In Saxony, in Württemberg, and elsewhere the Estates nevertheless strongly influenced the religious settlement. It was due to their efforts that the monastic revenues were not entirely dissipated, but partly used for pious and educational purposes. . . . Even in Bavaria the Estates strongly voiced their religious demands at the diet; and thanks to their efforts the chalice was for some time conceded to the laity. In the secularized duchy of Prussia the Estates emerged as the decisive power. . . . They dominated the Church and the administration and made the duke completely dependent on them-

selves, playing him off against the king of Poland and becoming the real masters of the country. Nor did the princes of the other Lutheran principalities gain much from the Reformation and their new position as the heads of the Church, contrary to the opinion which is usually held. Through lack of funds most princes were forced to sell the church lands very quickly, and the Estates used the ever-repeated demands for money to gain new privileges and some say in church affairs. They became the real defenders of orthodox Lutheranism. With the exception of Catholic Bavaria, their position everywhere became stronger in the course of the sixteenth century.

This growing strength of the Estates rested partly on the officials employed by them and on the machinery they developed, especially on their committees. It is true that the princes preferred to negotiate with a small committee rather than with the whole diet; but the diet only met from time to time, and meanwhile some machinery was required to deal with taxation and other current financial affairs and to safeguard the Estates' rights. The princes naturally would have liked the committees to vote them taxes and thus to be spared the expense and the opposition likely to emanate from a diet, but these attempts were everywhere strongly resisted by the Estates. They insisted on preserving intact their power of the purse and refused to empower their committees to make any money grants. Only after their opposition had been broken were the Bavarian Estates persuaded to depart from this principle and thus to accelerate their own decline. Those of other prinicipalities, such as Saxony and Württemberg, steadfastly refused to do so and thus preserved their powers.

The machinery provided by the Estates for administrative tasks was efficient and inexpensive, for the number of officials they employed was small, and many of their own members served in an honorary capacity, or for a purely nominal salary. . . . Knowledge of local affairs was another asset which the Estates possessed in contrast with their rulers' "foreign" officials. All the appointments, however, soon became vested in the Estates' committees which also co-opted their own new members, with or without the confirmation of the prince, so that the whole structure assumed the aspect of a narrow oligarchy dominated by some leading families. It is certainly true that the Estates — whether the Junkers of the east or the burghers of Württemberg — acted in the interests of the class which they represented, that their horizon was narrow, and that they did not stand for liberty in the modern sense of the term. Still, in defending their liberties and in raising their grievances, for example in matters of trade or against princely monopolies, they often defended the true interests of the country against the prince and his officials. In complaining about heavy labour and carrying services and the great damage caused by deer and other wild animals they championed the interests of the peasants. In opposing forcible recruiting and too heavy military burdens they prevented some of the worst excesses of petty despotism. Neither can it truly be maintained that the Estates were not willing to undertake permanent duties, nor that they were "impervious to the needs of the modern state," that the organization of the administration remained stationary where they predominated. In many principalities the Estates developed new administrative organs, especially in the field of finance. In some they introduced the first indirect taxes in place of the antiquated and less suitable direct taxes. The mixed "deputations" of Württemberg associated the Estates with the new organs of administration and thus provided a link between them and the state. Many members of the Estates served the state willingly, and their grants were often very liberal.

These remarks also show that another common criticism of the Estates is not really justified: that they did not create anything new, but had an entirely negative function. Thus Professor Hartung in his standard constitutional history of Germany wrote only a few years ago:

The Estates resisted burdens and wrongs imposed by the princes, but they created nothing new. As a rule they were satisfied if they need not pay any taxes, if the prince's officials were not permitted to penetrate into their domains and were firmly bound to observe the country's liberties. . . . Even when the Estates raised higher demands and . . . aimed at a share in the government, their aims remained more negative than positive. They wanted to limit the prince, to prevent him from taking measures which might damage their own interests. . . . They did not think of permanently influencing the government, they were the defenders of medieval autonomy. . . .

With regard to Württemberg and the policy of the dukes in the eighteenth century he goes even further and declares: "There is no doubt that this absolutist tendency, the references to the changed times, to the *salus publica*, which demanded a departure from the letter of the old treaties, were justified. . . ."

In other words, the tendency to denigrate the German Estates and to side with the princes, who tried to suppress them, persists to the present day. This tendency has always been so pronounced that fifty years ago a German historian exclaimed: "It is unjustified simply to take on all occasions the side of the absolute state against the Estates. . . ." But his voice has remained a cry in the wilderness. Recently, however, Professor Hartung has admitted that the Estates "formed, through their mere existence, a counter-weight to absolute government and therewith kept alive the idea of liberty. The liberal movement of the nineteenth century was able to link up with this inheritance, most clearly and most directly in Württemberg. . . ." Surely, this consideration alone ought to lead to a revision of the one-sided attitude towards the Estates. It is no accident, surely, that the liberal movement of the nineteenth century was strongest in those areas of Germany where the Estates survived the period of absolute government. Not only the idea of liberty, but the principles of self-government were kept alive by the Estates, as the Freiherr vom Stein so clearly perceived in Cleves and Mark. That this tradition did not die out in Germany was due to the opposition of the Estates to petty despotism and to the preconceived uniformity, which was the ideal of all absolute governments.

*   *   *

From a position of great strength which they occupied in the sixteenth century most of the German Estates declined in the seventeenth century; indeed, as we have seen, the Estates of Bavaria already in the sixteenth century. The causes of this rapid decline, especially in the later seventeenth century, have been discussed by many historians. The growth of princely power has been attributed to the adoption of primogeniture and the cessation of the many partitions, which in the fifteenth century played into the hands of the Estates. Yet the hundred and fifty years after the adoption of the *Dispositio Achillea*[1] in Brandenburg were the period of the Estates' greatest power; and in Württemberg there followed upon the acceptance of the same principle the deposition of Duke Eberhard and the treaty of Tübingen, and then the consolidation of the Estates' influence in the second half of the sixteenth century. With the exceptions of Bavaria and Hesse, a similar consolidation occurred at that time in most other principalities. This also disposes of another argument which has often been put forward: that the growth of princely power was due to the Reformation, the new position of the Protestant prince as the *summus episcopus* of his lands, and the strength he gained through

the dissolution of the monasteries. But the German princes benefited but little from the spoliation of the Church. The victory of the dukes of Bavaria over their Estates, on the other hand, was connected with the advance of the Counter-Reformation, the financial and political backing the dukes were given by the clergy, and the activities of the Jesuits in favour of the Catholic princes. So, fifty years later, were the victories of the Habsburgs over the Estates of Austria, Bohemia, Moravia, and Silesia, whose powers rivalled those of the crown in the period before the outbreak of the Thirty Years War.

The Thirty Years War certainly marked a decisive change in the fortunes of the Estates in many German territories. But, as we have seen, in Cleves and Mark, Hesse-Cassel, Saxony, and Württemberg the Estates' influence actually increased as a result of the war. Only where their leaders were Protestants, and the princes Catholics, did the military victories of the Counter-Reformation result in a defeat of the Estates and their policy of religious liberty. Elsewhere the issue was much more complex. Nor can it be maintained that after 1648 the Estates were "rotting from inside" (*innerlich morsch*), that there was no need to defeat them, that they withered away without any great effort on the part of the princes, and that sharp conflicts between prince and Estates only occurred as an exception. The preceding pages and the sharp clashes which occurred in Brandenburg and Prussia provide ample proof that this was not the case. Even in the Habsburg territories the Estates, in spite of their defeat in the Thirty Years War, showed a surprising tenacity and survived into the later eighteenth century.

As a result of the Thirty Years War and of the wars against Louis XIV standing armies came into being in many parts of Germany. . . .

Drawn into the struggles for power, often against their will, many German princes sought to imitate the example of the most powerful king in Europe, who

[1] The *Dispositio Achillea* was the "family law" promulgated by Albrecht Achilles, Margrave of Brandenburg, in 1473. By that law Albrecht, who had earlier united Kalinbach and Aurbach, divorced his frankish lands from his Brandenburg lands as part of his unifying activities. [Editor's note]

possessed the largest forces and carried
everything before him. Louis XIV was
strong, and he was absolute, the leading
protagonist of the theory of the Divine
Right of Kings and of the practice of absolute government. In their endeavours to
establish a standing army most princes met
with the opposition of their Estates, who
rightly pointed to the extreme exhaustion
of the country after the ravages of the
Thirty Years War and to the need of re-
cuperation. Thus a conflict became almost
inevitable.

*   *   *

. . . The power of resistance of the nobility and the towns was sapped by social
and economic changes, by the price revolution, and especially by the Thirty Years
War. After its end recovery took a long
time, for war continued in the west, in the
south-east, and in the north during the
second half of the seventeenth century,
and war benefited the princes and the
growth of their armies. If the seventeenth
century had not been so belligerent, so
filled with struggles for power, the strength
of the German Estates might have persisted. The power policy of the time favoured the growth of princely authority,
not only in Germany. Faced with the
power of Louis XIV the methods of the
Estates seemed as antiquated as was the
militia, which they favoured, against the
might of the French army.

The struggles between princes and Estates had much in common with the conflicts between crown and Parliament, but
the outcome was usually the opposite.
Thanks to the prevalence of the gentry in
the House of Commons and its close links
with the urban merchants and lawyers, the
House of Commons possessed a social
homogeneity which, in Germany, only
existed in Württemberg. It also existed in
the diets of Poland and of Hungary, which
were entirely dominated by the landed
nobility. The sharp social and economic
conflicts, the antagonism and the rigid
separation of nobility and towns, which

were so characteristic of Germany and
other continental countries, did not exist in
the English Parliament, partly thanks to
the fact that the knights of the shire and
the burgesses sat together in one house.
Even the House of Lords, thanks to the
specific traits of the English peerage, was
not separated by a gulf from the Lower
House: in many ways the interests of the
nobility were identical with those of the
landed gentry who dominated the Commons and whose members might be ele-
vated to the peerage; while the younger
sons of peers often sat in the Commons.
The two groups were connected by many
family ties and common economic interests.
Their members co-operated harmoniously
as Justices of the Peace and in other functions of local government, which provided
a firm basis for their activities in Parliament. In practice the nobility and the gentry formed one ruling group. Some members of the House of Lords were strongly
drawn towards Puritan ideas, and in the
seventeenth century some worked together
with Puritan members of the House of
Commons in commercial and colonizing
ventures. In the critical hour of the Long
Parliament a minority of the peers joined
hands with the majority of the Commons
in united opposition to the king. In the
weapon of Puritanism they possessed an
ideology and an organization, a burning
faith, which were entirely lacking in Germany, even where Lutheran Estates opposed a Calvinist or a Catholic prince.

No German prince carefully nurtured
the Estates as Henry VIII did; no German
prince deliberately increased the Estates'
privileges; no German prince went out of
his way to seek the Estates' support against
the Pope or against foreign enemies. A
leading authority on English constitutional
history under the Tudors has written:

It is remarkable that in the Tudor period
— the period of despotic government — there
should have been steady progress in the development and definition of the privilege of
Parliament. The explanation is to be found
not in the strength of Parliament but in its

weakness. It was the Tudor policy to rule by means of Parliament because the Tudor sovereigns were not afraid of Parliament.

In the sixteenth century the powers of many German Estates, in the fields of finance, foreign policy, and military affairs, were considerably greater than those of the English Parliament. They had their own officials and their permanent committees, functioning even when the diet was not in session and during the intervals between one diet and the next, and they dominated the financial administration of the principality. Yet they exercised no judicial functions, hence could not wield the weapon of impeachment, and their privileges were less well-defined than those of Parliament. The German princes, on the other hand, were much weaker than the Tudors, internally as well as externally, continuously threatened by other princes and by the Emperor. They could not possibly follow the same course as the Tudors and strengthen their Estates. They were afraid of them, hence they sought to curtail their powers, although in the sixteenth century they were successful in doing so only in Bavaria. The German Estates, in spite of their great powers in the financial field, only with much hesitation used the weapon of grievances before supply. They easily granted money against fair promises, without a guarantee that they would ever be fulfilled. Many princes were able to disregard solemn undertakings, to violate the Estates' privileges, to levy taxes without their consent. Hardly any Estates thought of resisting by force such infringements of the constitution; at most they would appeal to the courts of the Empire, hoping for protection by the Emperor or a foreign ruler. Perhaps it was the teaching of passive obedience by Luther and other churchmen which prevented opposition from crystallizing into resistance. Even the Estates of Württemberg did not dream of opposing the duke by force of arms. The "conspiracy" of the Bavarian noblemen against Duke Albert V was largely a fabrication of the government. Here lies one of the decisive differences between the attitude of the English Parliament and that of the German Estates.

The great struggles between Royalists and Parliamentarians found little echo in Germany. Only in the duchy of Cleves, where the Estates maintained close connexions with the States General of the United Provinces and were animated by the spirit of Calvinism, was a comparison made between the aims of the Estates and the opposition of Parliament to Charles I. It was not the Estates, however, who claimed the title of Parliamentarians, but the Electoral government which accused them of such ambitions, presumably to blacken them in the eyes of their friends among the Dutch Estates. Likewise in the duchy of Calenberg, when the Estates made difficulties about granting supply, it was the chancellor who in 1651 asserted that "the principles of the Puritans became widespread in Germany," not the Estates who claimed this relationship. In reality, however, the spirit of the Roundheads was singularly absent from seventeenth-century Germany. Perhaps some of the stronger towns, such as Königsberg or Wesel, came closest to offering armed resistance to the Great Elector of Brandenburg, who to them was a foreign prince and represented alien interests. But a show of force, the arrest of their leaders, was sufficient to reduce them to obedience. There was no London and no Paris to oppose the king, but only small, declining towns, with an anxious spirit and few resources. Königsberg might hope for help from the king of Poland, Wesel for aid from the States General, but none was rendered. The nobility was not animated by the spirit of the Fronde, nor by that of the Huguenots, but by that of loyalty to their prince whom they were eager to serve. The nobility and the towns were bitterly hostile to each other. No revolutionary movement could arise under such conditions.

Yet the German Estates fulfilled important historical functions. Their traditions remained alive, especially in the southwest of Germany. Their opposition may not have been very effective, but it existed nevertheless. They preserved the spirit of constitutional government and liberty in the age of absolute monarchy. In many principalities they showed great vitality, even in the eighteenth century. A new spirit began to permeate them with the coming of the French Revolution and the penetration of French ideas of liberty and equality. For these reasons alone the Estates deserve an honoured place in German history. They did not reach the great eminence of the English Parliament or of the Dutch Estates. But in many principalities they retained their influence much

longer than the representative institutions of other European countries, especially those of France and Spain. It has been said of the Estates of Cleves and Mark that in the struggle with the Great Elector of Brandenburg they "more than once . . . stood for the principles of the modern state." This can be maintained in a more general sense and with equal justification of the Estates of Württemberg and of Saxony, of the duchy of Prussia and of other German principalities. Germany is a country of many different traditions. One of them, and not the least important, was kept alive by the strenuous opposition of the Estates to the principles of absolute government.

THE "NEW MONARCHY" IN SWEDEN

CARL INGVAR ANDERSSON

Dr. Andersson, born in 1899, has had a distinguished career as an historian and as Royal Archivist of Sweden. His mastery of Swedish history has been shown in his *Sveriges historia* or *History of Sweden*, from which the present article was taken. In addition to general works, including his *Introduction to Sweden*, Dr. Andersson has published a number of studies on sixteenth century Swedish history, culminating in his *Erik XIV*, a recognized classic of Swedish historical writing.

T HE Regent, Gustav Eriksson Vasa, was now in a fair way to accomplishing what the Stures had so often attempted but only partially achieved. Taking advantage of the circumstances, notably Denmark's internal crisis and Lübeck's firm support, he had succeeded in detaching Sweden from the Union. Moreover, like Engelbrekt before him, Gustav looked beyond the old frontiers and undertook the conquest of Bohuslän, Blekinge, and

Skåne, ruling for a period over the first two. So far, however, three of the most important Swedish strongholds, Stockholm, Kalmar, and Älvsborg, were still in the hands of the Danes, and Finland too was largely controlled by Christian's supporters. Nevertheless it was anticipated that the ships and money from Lübeck would soon enable the Regent to win the rest of the kingdom.

The help given by Lübeck had certain

From Carl Ingvar Andersson, *History of Sweden*, translated from *Sveriges historia* by Carolyn Hannay (New York, 1956), pp. 120–131. Reprinted by permission of Frederick A. Praeger, Inc., and George Allen & Unwin Ltd.

important consequences. The "honourable council" which governed the town was naturally anxious that the capital it had invested in Scandinavian politics should be firmly guaranteed. This was impossible, however, until Sweden possessed a settled and recognized government, and that meant, in effect, a king. A *Riksdag*, attended by delegates from Lübeck, met in Strängnäs at Whitsuntide 1523, and Gustav Eriksson Vasa was elected King of Sweden. The Lübeck counsellors were placed at the right hand of the new King during the ceremony in the Cathedral and shortly afterwards Gustav Vasa and his Council (which had now been reconstructed) granted certain very favourable trading rights to Lübeck and its allies. The Hansa merchants had thus proved successful in their speculation, and they no doubt hoped that they would find in the young King a willing tool.

The Danes had already evacuated Älvsborg before the election of Gustav Vasa, and within a few weeks he controlled the capital. On Midsummer Day he rode through the south gate into the sorely ravaged Stockholm, where "he was received and admitted with great ceremony, with pomp and circumstance, as was meet." At the beginning of July Kalmar Castle surrendered to one of Gustav Vasa's principal commanders, the German nobleman Berend von Melen, and in due course Finland, too, was conquered. Relations of a kind were established with Denmark and her new ruler, Frederick I; Sweden was repulsed in her attempt to conquer Gotland, and by degrees Denmark recovered the frontier provinces that Sweden had annexed; the last to go was Bohuslän, which Gustav Vasa retained until the beginning of the 1530's.

Nothwithstanding all that had been achieved, however, the security of the throne was more apparent than real. The strength of Gustav Vasa's position in Sweden depended primarily on the willing support of the various localities, and this could not always be relied upon. The policy of the Stures had favoured licence and brutality in the countryside, and the forces which had supported Gustav Vasa might easily be deflected by a change of circumstances or mood. Again, the King had achieved his position with the support of the Sture party, and that party might well hold the view that, in ascending the throne and accepting the help of Lübeck, he had usurped the place which belonged by right to one of Sten Sture's young sons. Equally unpredictable was the attitude of the nobles and the Church, both of them forces over and above the provincial authorities. Nor was the King's task made any easier by the fact that both he and the kingdom were indebted to Lübeck, especially as he had inherited from his predecessors in the late Middle Ages the problem of making both ends meet in his treasury. Consequently the first few decades of Gustav Vasa's rule were a period of recurring crises which, with their intrigues, their violence, and their trickery vividly illustrated the methods of the Renaisance era.

The first crisis was precipitated by discontent among the old adherents of the Sture party. Peder Jakobsson Sunnanväder, possibly Sten Sture's chief adviser, was again in Sweden, and it was not long before he had fallen foul of the King. Early in 1524 Sten's widow, Christina Gyllenstierna, returned from captivity in Denmark, eager to re-enter the political arena. Supported by the Admiral Sören Norby, Christian II's last faithful follower in Scandinavia, she intrigued against the man who had ousted her sons from the position she had hoped would be theirs. The fractious population of Dalarna were complaining of the high cost of living and the shortage of salt, and these grievances were fully exploited by Peder Sunnanväder, Christina Gyllenstierna, and several of Sten's former retainers. The King was also causing dissatisfaction by his apparent interest, exaggerated by rumour, in the new and disturbing doctrines preached by the Lutheran reformers, principally the

Swede Olaus Petri. Norby was campaigning in the south to reinstate Christian II, while the King chose just this moment to quarrel with his commander Berend von Melen. Nevertheless he weathered the storm. Sören Norby was defeated in Skåne, Christina Gyllenstierna was forced to surrender, and Peder Sunnanväder fled to Norway; Berend von Melen retired to Germany, and many of the soldiers he left behind were executed. A skilful blend of threats and cajolery temporarily restored order in Dalarna, and the King later won a symbolic victory over the Sture party by capturing Peder Sunnanväder and his ally Master Knut. His chronicler, Peder Svart, relates how they were led into Stockholm, "clad in old, threadbare tattered cloaks, riding backwards on famished horses, Peder Sunnanväder with a coronet of straw on his head and a broken wooden sword by his side, Master Knut with a crosier of birch-bark." Both men were sentenced to death and executed.

Meanwhile, a fresh rising was threatening in Dalarna and Värmland, led by an enigmatic figure who is known in Swedish history as the *Daljunkare*. He claimed that he was Sten Sture's son Nils, who died about this time, but Gustav Vasa declared that he was a farmhand and an impostor. Whatever his real identity, he was supported by the Norwegian aristocracy, with whom he was on intimate terms, and by members of the old Sture party. The grievances of his adherents in Dalarna centred on the taxes imposed by the King, the new "Lutheranism," and the recent fashion for "slashed and scalloped garments"; and although Gustav Vasa replied in his plausible way that the taxation was to defray the debts of the country, that he had ordained nothing but the preaching of God's word and the Gospel, and that the new fashions harmed none but those who adopted them, the disturbances continued, and the time-honoured name of Sture proved well able to hold its own against the new name of Vasa. The King had simultaneously to cope with the uncurbed defiance of the

peasants, the demands of Lübeck for a speedy repayment, and an unstable situation in the field of foreign affairs. Yet he did not lose heart. During these critical years he and his followers undertook an extensive reorganization of administration and finances, revealing in the process both his undaunted optimism and his remarkable foresight. Harassed though he was by risings and conspiracies, Gustav Vasa strove to put into practice the system of centralization which had been conceived by the Stures, aiming first and foremost at freeing himself from his dependence on Lübeck and secondly at the provision of loyal troops. He found support among the burgesses of the towns, whom he in his turn treated favourably, and also among the reforming clergy and certain groups of the nobility. Moreover, not all the provinces were as fractious as Dalarna — provided, at least, that the King would grant some of their economic demands and ensure supplies of salt.

Sten Sture the Younger, who had been in a similar position, had already fallen foul of the leaders of the Church ten years earlier. If clashes were easy enough then, they were still more so now, when Lutheranism was being preached by Olaus Petri and other Swedish theologians who had been trained at Wittenberg. Gustav Vasa, as a practical man, soon saw the possible connection between the new teaching and the political concepts he had inherited from the Stures. The Catholic Church was the only rich corporate body in the country, and if the King was to subdue the *Daljunkare* and stabilize the finances, he must have its property at his disposal. It was calculated that by the end of the Middle Ages the Church owned 21.3 per cent. of the Swedish homesteads (as against 20.7 per cent. held by the nobles, 5.6 per cent. by the crown, and 52.4 per cent. by the tax peasants[1]; it should, however, be

[1] Tax peasants (*skattebönder*) *owned* the land they farmed and paid a *public* tax, not a private rent, to the crown. Crown peasants (*kronobönder*) who *rented* their land from the crown were

noted that in Finland, where nobility and Church had not achieved so strong a position, tax peasants' land amounted to over 96 per cent. of the whole). Although the leading churchman, Bishop Hans Brask of Linköping, had been a supporter of Gustav Vasa, it was not long before the two were on bad terms. The King irritated the bishops and the monasteries by his demands for loans and the maintenance of soldiers; and his Chancellor, Laurentius Andreae, who held Lutheran views, prophesied the speedy downfall of those who had previously held great power. It was evident that a crisis was at hand; and in 1527, while the rising of the *Daljunkare* was going on, the representatives of the four Estates were summoned to a *Riksdag* in Västerås.

The meeting was attended by delegates from Lübeck, who endorsed the King's pronouncement that discontented members could themselves negotiate with the Lübeck creditors and see "whether they wished to be paid with rebellion." In the royal proclamations which were read before the Estates, Gustav Vasa affirmed that *he* had fulfilled all his obligations to the people, but that the *people* had not responded in kind. The revenues, he declared, were insufficient for the country's needs. The nobles had been weakened as a result of the loss of most of their estates, either by will or donation, to the Church and the monasteries, and they were demanding compensation in the form of crown fiefs. The King in turn pointed out that since the revenue was already inadequate, he was unable to meet their demands. His statement culminated in a request that he should be allowed to abdicate, leaving the Estates to overcome the difficulties as best they could.

The King argued his case with a skill which was well calculated to sway the opinions of the nobles. The fault was (though he did not reveal it at the time)

that his project for a centralized administration under his direct control was incompatible with the mediaeval system under which large fiefs were bestowed on the nobles, though he admitted that they were justified in asking aid or fiefs of the crown. He concluded his statement with a clear hint as to where the solution was to be found — namely in the Church — thereby putting into the nobles' mouths the answer he desired. With irrefutable logic he had linked together the new administrative system, the crown's need for increased income, and the demands of the nobles. Let the Church meet the crown's demands for money and the nobles' demands for fiefs and estates.

The nobles responded precisely in the manner he had intended. They made detailed proposals as to how the property and income of the Church should best be used for the benefit of the crown and the nobility, and they promised to support the King against all rebels. The other Estates — apart from the clergy, who had no voice in the matter — agreed with the nobles in all essentials, and the decisions were enacted in the famous *Riksdag* decree known as the Västerås *Recess*. The castles owned by the bishops were to be handed over to the King, who was also to determine the number of soldiers they should maintain. The surplus revenues of the bishops, the cathedrals, and the canons were to be regularly paid to the King in cash. The monasteries were to be handed over intact as fiefs to the nobles. Moreover the nobles were to be permitted on certain conditions to reclaim the estates which they had given to the Church since the middle of the fifteenth century. In a later statute, the Västerås *Ordinantia,* the power of the State over the Church was established in a manner which paved the way for further progress along the lines laid down in the Västerås *Recess*.

Gustav Vasa had thus shrewdly got the Estates exactly where he wanted them. The representatives of the Church were powerless against the unanimity of the

---

similar in status and rights to those who rented their lands from lords (*frälsebönder*) or from the Church; they could not be said to own the homesteads they cultivated.

nobles, burgesses, and peasants; and in the following years the acquisition by the State of Church revenues brought about a reduction in ecclesiastical property which affected even the parishes. Having achieved this great victory over the Church's powerful "State within a State" — a victory which he did not fail ruthlessly to exploit — Gustav Vasa was able to press on towards his great goal: the replacement of the existing loose federation of families, parishes, and provinces by a centralized administration. The nobility's demand for fiefs had been satisfied for the moment at the expense of the Church, and the administrative reforms could be undertaken with little fear of opposition from the aristocracy.

Moreover the King was now certain of the unconditional support of the Estates for any step he might take against the *Daljunkare*. Having summoned the rebels to him at Tuna, he treated them without mercy. The *Daljunkare's* chief agents were executed, and "when the others saw the blood begin to flow, then they changed their tune; they were sorely afraid, lifted up their voices and wept, fell on their knees, praying and beseeching mercy of the King, in God's name." Thus did Gustav Vasa himself persuade his chronicler Peder Svart to describe the great reckoning which followed the Västerås decisions. Finally the *Daljunkare* himself, who had fled to Germany, was captured and executed.

It had also been decreed at the Västerås *Riksdag* that God's word should purely and plainly be proclaimed in the kingdom — a somewhat vague formulation, which left open for the present the spiritual aspect of the Church question but which allowed full scope for the propagation of Lutheran doctrine. There was as yet no question of a final break with the Pope. But even before the Västerås meeting Olaus Petri had published in Swedish a book of sacred songs which were strongly Lutheran in tone (several of them, incidentally, sung to-day in J. O. Wallin's revised versions); and five years later, in 1531, he drew up

some of the fundamental doctrines of Lutheranism which summarize the finest features of the early Swedish Reformation: "We in Sweden also belong to God, as do other nations, and the tongue we have has been given to us by God. . . ." Mass should therefore be celebrated in Swedish. But he also urged another fundamental principle, that of toleration: "Let none be constrained or forced to attend the Swedish service . . . in the same way as none can be forced to God's word; freely and unconstrainedly must it be accepted, if it is to bear fruit." After the Västerås *Riksdag* it became clear that there was an impassable gulf between the members of the old Church and the young and ruthless Statebuilder, and Gustav Vasa's erstwhile faithful counsellor, Bishop Hans Brask, soon left the country, never to return.

But all was not yet plain sailing for the King and the new monarchy. The peasants, conservative by nature, were suspicious of the innovations in the Church and, if they found the right leaders, were still capable of breaking out. And although the Sture party was defeated, leaders might still be found. Some bold churchman might try and retrieve the losses of Västerås; and although a large number of the nobility had supported the King's policy on account of the advantages they were offered, there were still representatives of the old aristocracy who, realizing what the outcome must be, preferred to join forces with the Church. After all, the demagogic methods which Gustav Vasa had inherited from the Stures could equally well be used against him. The most prominent of these lords was Ture Jönsson Tre Rosor, who had had many years of political experience. In 1529, with the assistance of Bishop Magnus of Skara, he incited the peasantry of Småland and, more particularly, Västergötland to rise against the King; and the rebellion threatened to spread to Östergötland and Hälsingland. The state of affairs in the Church offered suitable material for propaganda, and for a time Gustav Vasa was really anxious. Once again fortune smiled on him, however, and the rising was put down by a combination of violence, subterfuge, and persuasion. Some of the leaders were executed, others fled the country. The victory of Västerås was now complete.

Shortly after this, in 1530, the King decreed that one bell in every church should be sacrificed to the exchequer. At first the decree applied only to the towns and monasteries, but the following year it was extended to include the country churches. This constituted a heartless attack on ancient beliefs; the bells, which called the congregation to worship and purified the air of evil spirits, had played a significant part in the religious life of the people ever since the time when they had first pealed forth from steeple and belfry during the great period of church-building in the early Middle Ages. In Bergslagen and Dalarna the King's agents were received with sledge-hammers, and driven away. To add to his difficulties, in 1531-2 Christian II launched an expedition to Norway in an attempt to recover his kingdoms; his retinue included both Gustav Trolle, an exile for the past ten years, and the leaders who had escaped from the Västergötland rising. The fourth crisis, "the Bell Rebellion," was under way — Gustav Vasa had to face such situations with curious regularity during this first period of his reign. However, King Christian was taken prisoner; and at Kopparberget, in February 1533, Gustav Vasa settled his accounts with the unruly men of Dalarna for the third and last time. His reprisals were more ruthless than ever before. Among the spokesmen of the malcontents were men who had supported him at the beginning of his career. They, like the other leaders, were condemned to death. Gustav Vasa's feelings at being forced to demand the blood of his old friends were never revealed. At all events, the sentences were duly carried out, and thus the most recalcitrant province in the country was completely subdued. The King's path was certainly bloody; but it led him to his goal.

By this time Gustav Vasa had completed in all essentials the reorganization of the administration. Many of the mediaeval fiefs, which had been used by the aristocracy to further their individual interests, had already been largely incorporated into the new system, which was closely supervised by the King, his Chancery and Treasury. The nobles who had controlled those fiefs which contained royal castles were replaced by bailiffs, dependent on the central government. Gustav Vasa had throughout been favoured by circumstances, and many of the chief nobles had died during the early years of his reign; this social class had been further undermined by the failure of the Västergötland rising. There was no younger generation equipped to safeguard the interests of the higher aristocracy, and the remaining members had been placated by the decline in the power of the Church. The reform of the administration could thus proceed without any very serious opposition. Gustav Vasa was certainly the right man for the task. His own upbringing as a landowner stood him in good stead, and he had also learnt much from the Stures, from the excellent estate management of the Church and from Lübeck. He reformed the assessment and collection of the land taxes, and reorganized the various uses to which the natural products they yielded could be put. Further, a comprehensive survey was made of the entire revenues of the crown in ready money and in kind for the years 1530 and 1533 — an unprecedented achievement. The King personally supervised all the work of the government, carrying on a profitable trade with the crowns' levies of oxen, butter, and grain, and using them to ensure supplies to different parts of the country. In this he was able to anticipate local shortage and famine, thereby removing one of the standard grievances. The increasing appropriation of the Church's property and revenue lightened the burden of taxation and helped to improve the crown's financial position; and the King was now able to attract capable men into his service by the offer of good rewards. By these means a centralized state was being established on modern lines; and the increased power of the King was further manifested in the success of his policy of emancipating the Swedish Church from Rome, a process which was completed during the 1530's.

On many occasions during the first fifteen years of his reign it had seemed as though the King must give up. He had constantly been forced to use the threat of abdication as a weapon against the intractable peasantry with whom he treated in market place and assembly — above all at the Västerås *Riksdag*, where the prospect hung over the proceedings like a sword of Damocles. But in fact he had no intention of surrendering. He had already identified himself with his kingdom, which he ruled as to the manner born. The weakening of Lübeck's hold on him, however, he owed partly to external circumstances. The end of the first phase of his reign had seen the origin in Denmark of a domestic crisis known as the *Greve* (Count's) Feud — so called after the Count of Oldenburg, who had commanded a strong army of merce-

naries from Lübeck and elsewhere against Duke Christian, subsequently Christian III of Denmark. The Swedish King saw in this feud his chance of settling with Lübeck, and he intervened on Christian's side (they were brothers-in-law married to two sisters). He did not win all he had hoped for, but the reverses suffered by Lübeck considerably strengthened Sweden's position against the town which, by virtue of the 1523 privileges, dominated her foreign trade. Lübeck still retained a powerful control over Swedish trade, but her political decline was in Sweden's favour.

Thus Gustav Vasa had swept aside the three main obstacles to his goal — the Church, provincial self-government, and Lübeck. Unrest in the country had been stamped out and the administration was being given its last touches. The King was putting into practice the system which the Stures had envisaged for Sweden. The question now was: should he stop at this point, or could he — dare he, indeed — go further?

PARLIAMENTARY MONARCHY

ROBERT HOWARD LORD

The late Professor Robert Howard Lord was born in 1885. He was a gradu-
ate student at Harvard, where he took a Ph.D. in 1910, writing *The Second
Partition of Poland*, a book that has since remained a standard work on the
problem. His interest in diplomatic history led to several other books, including *The Origins of the War of 1870* and *Three Peace Conferences*, written in
co-operation with Charles D. Hazen and William Roscoe Thayer. *Some Problems of the Peace Conference*, written with Charles Homer Haskins, was representative of Lord's interest in the traditions of political freedom in Modern
Europe, an interest also shown by the present paper, first presented as an address before the Catholic Historical Association, December 28, 1929.

Iᴛ is generally agreed that one of the greatest achievements of the Middle Ages was the development of the representative system and of parliaments. It is largely, though perhaps not sufficiently, recognized that in the general scheme of the evolution of European states, between the age of feudalism and the era of absolute monarchy, there intervenes a period of what may be called parliamentary monarchy, of quasi-constitutionalism, of experiments — practically for the first time in history — with representative institutions. This period extends roughly from the thirteenth to the seventeenth century. The hallmark of it is the fact that the power of the crown was then more or less extensively limited by that of assemblies, in part elective, whose members, though directly and immediately representing only the politically active classes, were also regarded as representing in a general way the whole population of the land. But the historians who have treated of the representative institutions of this period have usually confined their studies to one or two or three countries. In America and Britain atten-

tion has been centered almost entirely on the English Parliament, the French States-General, or the Spanish Cortes. What has not been adequately recognized, in the first place, is the universality of the phenomenon. The fact is that class-parliaments or assemblies of estates arose not merely in the three kingdoms of the British Isles, but in all the realms of the Iberian peninsula, in France and all the French provinces, in the Holy Roman Empire and in nearly all the territorial states of Germany, the Netherlands, and Italy, in the Scandinavian kingdoms, Hungary, Bohemia, Poland, and Muscovy. Except for the municipal republics of Germany and Italy, where assemblies of estates were obviously out of the question, and the Balkan lands, where the Turkish conquest cut short the natural course of development, parliaments are found in this period in every state in Europe from Scotland to Hungary and from Portugal to Russia.

These hundreds of parliaments, national and provincial, ought to be studied comparatively, if we are ever to have an adequate conception of the constitutional de-

From Robert Howard Lord, "The Parliaments of the Middle Ages and Early Modern Period," *Catholic Historical Review*, XVI (1930), pp. 125–144. Reprinted by permission of the *Catholic Historical Review*.

velopment of Europe as a whole, and not simply a set of generalizations based on the history of three or four of the larger countries. But no such comparative study has ever been made. From the lack of it many misconceptions have arisen: e. g., that the English Parliament was in nearly every respect unique, or that England was the only country in Europe that developed a vigorous and effective parliamentary system, or that England alone preserved its parliament uninterruptedly from the Middle Ages down to the nineteenth century.

In a paper like this it is obviously impossible to enter into any detailed treatment of so vast a field. But since no one has yet undertaken to present even a brief comparative survey of the whole group of European parliaments of that age, from Edinburgh and Lisbon to Moscow, perhaps it may be of interest to make that attempt here.

The assemblies in question went by various names: "Parliament," in England, Ireland, Scotland, Sicily, Naples, and the Papal States, and (for certain special assemblies) in Aragon, Catalonia, and Valencia (in Spanish and Italian *"Parlamento"*); *"Cortes"* for the ordinary parliaments of Portugal and the Spanish kingdoms; "States-General" and "Provincial Estates" in France and the Netherlands; *"Stati"* in Piedmont, but *"Congregazioni generali"* for the estates representing the whole of the territories of the House of Savoy; *"Reichstag"* in the Holy Roman Empire, and *"Landtag"* in the German territorial states; *"Rigsdag"* in Denmark and Norway; *"Riksdag"* in Sweden; *"Sněm"* and *"Sejm"* ("assemblies") in Bohemia and Poland respectively; *"Országgyülés"* and *"Zemski Sobor"* ("assemblies of the land") in Hungary and Russia — although for all the parliaments of Central and Northern Europe the custom of our language is to say "Diet."

These assemblies usually arose in that stage of political evolution when, amid the decay of feudalism, the prince, engaged in building up a more unified and more highly organized national or territorial state, but not yet strong enough to proceed as he liked, autocratically, felt the need of enlisting the support of the politically active classes of the population; when the nobles, no longer able to rule independently in their localities, might still hope by corporate organization and collective action to wield a large power over the common state; and when through the growth of cities a vigorous new social class had come to the front with important interests to defend and often with ambitions to have a voice in public affairs equal to that of the older privileged classes. Between the crown, on the one hand, and the leading social classes on the other, a certain equilibrium had been reached, and collaboration and mutual concessions were necessary. More concretely, it was the ever growing financial needs of the crown — the need of larger revenues than those supplied by the domain lands and the customary feudal aids — that usually conduced most powerfully to the calling of the first parliaments. Other factors that sometimes operated were: disputed successions to the throne (Denmark, Norway); foreign invasion (Scotland, Sweden); the desire of the princes for popular support against the magnates (Hungary, Russia), or against the Papacy (France, Portugal). The crown most commonly took the initiative in the introduction of these assemblies. But cases are not lacking in which the subjects (through "leagues," "confederations," "unions") forced a weak government or a tyrannical ruler to take them into organized consultation (Aragon, Bohemia, various German and Netherlands territories).

The practice of consultation through parliaments seems in most countries to have arisen from a development of the old *curia regis*. Medieval rulers were accustomed, for treating more important public affairs, to expand their ordinary "court" or "council" into a large assembly . . . which might be attended by most or all of the prelates, magnates, and tenants-in-chief, and in some countries by all the nobility.

It was natural that, with the urban renaissance, "men of the good towns" or other spokesmen of the commons should occasionally be called to these gatherings, when matters affecting them were to come up. In order that these sessions of the enlarged *curia regis* should be turned into parliaments, three things were necessary: (1) that the consultation of all the leading social classes, especially of the townsmen, should become regular and not remain purely sporadic; (2) that their mode of representation should assume fixed forms; and (3) that these assemblies, instead of being called merely to acclaim decisions already reached by the prince, should be admitted to an effective collaboration with him and to a certain measure of power and responsibility.

For some time, indeed, an alternative method of consulting the population was extensively practiced. Especially when it was a question of raising money, but often for other purposes as well, the crown would send its agents around the country to negotiate separately with the local communities or with certain social groups. Before long it was, of course, discovered that this procedure was cumbersome, slow, and uncertain: that the more effective plan would be, instead of having the representatives of the king go to the country, to have the representatives of the country come to the king. Nevertheless, long after central parliaments had been introduced, the crown continued in most countries occasionally to prefer the method of treating with each local community or with each class separately, for taxation especially. And in countries where the local assemblies had become strongly entrenched, they often served as organs for the election of deputies to the parliaments, which thus appeared as "concentrations of local machinery" (England, Poland, Hungary).

It is customary to date the establishment of medieval parliaments from the time when the commons, normally represented by the townsmen, first gained admission to the national or territorial assemblies. This procedure, though open to many objections, is justified in as far as the admission of the "third estate" was, indeed, the decisive step in the transformation of the older feudal and clerical assemblies into something that might pass for a representation of the whole population. Moreover, some use of dates is necessary if we are to have any coherent picture of the course of this "wave of parliamentarism," which slowly overspread the continent. Hence it may be permissible to draw up a chronological table showing the relative priority or tardiness of the various countries in the establishment of parliaments, taking as a rough criterion the dates at which elected deputies of the cities first began to be summoned more or less regularly to the national or territorial assemblies.

It is a vexed question precisely where assemblies of the three estates first appeared in Europe. One can find vague allusions to such gatherings as being held in Catalonia in 1064; in Navarre in 1134; in Aragon in 1162 or 1163; in Agenais in 1182; in Béarn in "the twelfth century"; in Savoy in "the middle of the twelfth century." Leaving out of account such uncertain beginnings, we may, using the criterion defined above, arrange the order in which something that may be called a parliament appears in the several more important European countries. . . .

In general, the wave seems to have started down around the Pyrenees — whether on the southern or on the northern side is not quite certain — in the later twelfth century. In the thirteenth century it overspread the Iberian peninsula, many Italian states, and perhaps southern France. Around 1300 it had reached the British Isles. In the fourteenth century it spread to nearly every province or territorial state of France, the Netherlands, and Germany (in the stronger states of Eastern Germany assemblies of estates appear even in the thirteenth century). The Scandinavian kingdoms, Hungary and Poland, developed their parliaments only in the last century of the Middle Ages; and in Russia, al-

though the great national assemblies called
Zemski Sobors begin apparently in 1550,
the presence in them of elected deputies of
the towns cannot be proved before 1613.

With the notable exception of England,
where class distinctions were relatively
weak and confused, virtually all the parliaments here in question were essentially assemblies of estates, organized to represent
primarily the leading social classes; and this
outstanding class-character is one of the
chief differences between them and modern parliaments. With respect to the classes
represented, however, some divergences of
practice are to be marked.

The clergy, usually considered "the first
estate," appear at some time in virtually all
the assemblies here considered. As a separate estate, however, they voluntarily
dropped out of the national parliament in
England (after the middle of the fourteenth century), Naples, Poland, Hungary,
and Castile, except in so far as, in the first
four countries named, the presence of the
prelates among the barons could be considered a representation of the whole clerical body. After the Reformation this estate
also vanished from the parliaments of most
of the Protestant German states, the Dutch
Republic, and (most of the time) Scotland.

Nobles and gentry ("barons," "lords,"
"knights," "serving men" — by whatsoever
name they might be called) were a class
almost invariably found in these assemblies,
although in the sixteenth century they drop
out in Castile, Württemberg, and some
minor territories.

The "burgesses of the good towns" were
another element that was almost never lacking. They ceased to attend the Polish Diet,
however, by the close of the sixteenth century; and in Bohemia, Moravia, and Hungary in the later years of the Old Régime
their rôle was reduced to such nullity that
they might as well have ceased to attend.

In contrast to the townsmen, the peasantry enjoyed representation only in a few
instances: in the French States-General, in
Switzerland, the Tyrol, Friesland, Norway,
Sweden, and (until 1627) Denmark.

In general, the representation of classes
was narrowest in Flanders, where the cities
seem from the first to have monopolized
the Diet; in Poland, where the nobility ultimately did virtually the same; and in
Castile, where after 1538 the Cortes was
left solely to the Third Estate (the cities).
At the other extreme stand the Swedish or
Norwegian Diets, and especially the
French States-General, which from the
later fifteenth century on, must be called
by far the most broadly representative of all
these assemblies.

The States-General in its later form
stands out not only because of the com-
pleteness with which all classes — clergy,
nobles, townsmen, and peasants — were
represented in it, but also because all
classes elected their delegates, and through
an electoral procedure more highly organized than in any other country, and
by what in the rural districts, at least,
amounted almost to universal suffrage. In
sharp contrast to this, for most parliaments
the rule was that election was practiced
only for the representation of the towns
and of the peasants (where these latter had
representatives). And even for the towns,
in many cases election was replaced by
the sending *ex officio* of certain municipal
dignitaries, or the choice of the town's
representatives by the municipal council,
or their designation by drawing lots, or
their more or less thinly disguised appointment by the crown. Where election did
exist, it was carried out with such an endless variety of rules and forms that generalizations about it are almost impossible.

The clergy were represented in most
medieval parliaments only by prelates sitting *jure suo*. Elected deputies representing the whole clerical body are found only
in a few instances, notably in the French
States-General and the Diets of Norway
and Sweden.

As for the nobility, most commonly
every member of this class had the right
to attend parliament. This was the rule in
Scotland, Portugal, all the Spanish kingdoms (except in Castile where only those

whom the crown summoned attended), nearly all the Provincial Estates of France and the Netherlands, the German *Landtag*, in the Scandinavian kingdoms, and in Naples and Sicily. The evils of such a system were numerous and patent. It resulted too often in swamping a parliament with hordes of poverty-stricken, ignorant, and turbulent country squires, ready to sell their lungs or their votes to the highest bidder, or else eager only to rush the assembly's business through at once or turn it over to a committee in order to get home as soon as possible. But so strong was the prejudice that all noblemen ought to have at least the right of attending, whether as a patriotic duty or in order to circumvent the schemes of the crown or the oligarchs, that the rival system of having the mass of the nobility represented by elected deputies could seldom prevail. It did prevail chiefly in countries too large to permit of the personal attendance of most noblemen. Apart from the well-known and not altogether analogous case of England and Ireland, where the gentry and freeholders chose the "knights of the shire" in the county court, the nobles of France came to elect their deputies to the States-General in *bailliage* assemblies; those of Hungary chose their representatives in parliament at their "county congregations"; those of Poland did the same in their "dietines"; those of East Prussia in their *Aemter* gatherings; and those of Muscovy in their *uiezd* assemblies. But all efforts to introduce this system in such large realms as Bohemia, Denmark, and Sweden-Finland failed.

In their forms of meeting and deliberating nearly all the parliaments here surveyed present great similarities. Almost everywhere the king or prince alone had the right of summoning the assembly. As a rule, the letters of convocation specified more or less clearly the matters to come up in the impending session, though the crown usually avoided this unpleasant necessity whenever it felt strong enough to do so. The place of meeting ordinarily depended only on the choice of the ruler. Almost any town large enough to accommodate such a gathering might serve; and sometimes meetings were even held in the open country, like the Polish Election Diets, the old Hungarian assemblies on the Rákos field, or the early *Parlamento* of Friuli on horseback on the plain of Campoformio. Regularity as to the time of meeting was also decidedly the exception. Although in nearly every country the estates frequently demanded and the rulers sometimes promised annual or biennial or triennial parliaments, such promises were not very strictly observed. Nevertheless, while in some countries (e. g., France, Denmark, Russia) the national assembly was called only rarely, and under exceptional circumstances, in most countries meetings were held rather frequently — every two or three years, or even annually.

The session was almost invariably opened by a speech from the throne, delivered to all the estates jointly, outlining the royal or princely propositions, which commonly centered around a demand for subsidies. After this the assembly usually broke up into the various "houses" or "estates" or "*curiae*" in which it was accustomed to deliberate. And on this matter of the division into houses, so all-important for the efficient working of a parliament, practice varied widely. Numerous examples can be cited for every system from one chamber up to four chambers.

An assembly consisting of only one house appears in Castile (after 1538) and in Flanders, since all orders except the cities had been eliminated, and in certain parliaments where all classes were accustomed to sit together in one chamber, although sometimes voting by estates — as in Scotland, Languedoc, Piedmont, and Naples.

Bicameralism, often regarded as one of those unique inventions or happy accidents that have made the fortune of England, was, in fact, practiced in many countries. It might arise through the disappearance of one of the three estates usually found in these assemblies: of the clergy (as in

most of the Protestant German territories
or the Diets of the Dutch Republic), or of
the nobility (e. g., in Württemberg).
Sometimes the upper classes might sit together as an upper house ("grand corps")
and the commoners as a lower chamber
("second corps"), as in various French Provincial Estates. The development in England, whereby the House of Lords grew
out of the old enlarged King's Council
(Magnum Concilium), and the House of
Commons out of the union in one chamber of the elected deputies of the shires
and boroughs, was closely paralleled in Poland and Hungary. In these latter realms
the Magnum Concilium reappears as the
Senate or Table of Magnates, composed
of prelates and high officials, while a lower
house, the Chamber or Table of Deputies,
was formed from the elected representatives of the nobility and cities (the urban
element, however, quickly disappearing in
Poland).

By far the commonest arrangement on
the continent was a division into three
houses. Usually it was — clergy, nobles,
and cities, as in Portugal, Navarre, Catalonia, Valencia, the States-General and
most Provincial Estates in France and in
the Netherlands, Sicily, many German
Diets, Denmark (after the elimination of
peasant deputies), and, apparently, Russia.
Elsewhere tricameralism arose from the
fact that while the clergy vanished as a
separate estate, the greater and the lesser
nobility formed distinct curiae (Bohemia,
Saxony, Silesia, East Prussia). The division of the German Imperial Diet into
three curiae, electors, princes, and cities,
was a somewhat analogous arrangement.

Finally, a four-chamber parliament
sometimes appears, representing either
clergy, magnates, lesser nobles, and cities
(as in Aragon, Austria, Styria, and Moravia), or clergy, nobles, towns, and peasants (as in Sweden, Norway, Denmark
down to 1627, and the Tyrol).

A division into three or four houses
greatly aggravated two other characteristic
weaknesses of the parliaments of that

period: the difficulty of agreeing as to how
valid decisions were to be arrived at, and
the widespread use of imperative mandates.

Almost everywhere it was long disputed
whether, as between the several estates or
chambers, unanimity was required in order
to pass a measure, whether two estates
could "bind" a third, or whether the commons must accept whatever the higher
orders agreed upon. Usually the rule prevailed that the consent of all the estates was
necessary — with resulting complications
when it was a question of bringing three
or four estates into line. Sometimes, however, the difficulty was avoided by provid-
ing that decisions should be reached by
majority vote of the parliament sitting together as a kind of committee of the whole.
This system, practiced, e. g., in Languedoc
and sometimes in the French States-General, usually favored the Third Estate, as
outnumbering all the rest. But occasionally
it worked out the other way, as in Bohemia,
where ultimately the towns were reduced
to having only a single collective vote: i. e.,
for parliamentary decisions all the cities of
the kingdom together counted for no more
than one poor country squire.

Even more difficult was the problem
within individual estates of establishing
majority rule. The old idea that, over and
above the ordinary feudal obligations, no
one could be bound to anything to which
he had not freely consented; the tradition
that single lords or provinces or cities
might bargain separately with the crown,
outside parliament and for a time even in
parliament; the extreme importance attached by the privileged classes to their
personal or local "liberties"; the danger of
troubles or even civil war if the majority
attempted to impose their will on strongly
reluctant colleagues; the principle of the
Roman law, Vota non sunt numeranda,
sed ponderanda[1] — all these things long
combined to uphold the idea that a majority vote need not necessarily carry a
measure, that the opposition of a consider-

---

[1] Votes are not merely to be counted; they must be
weighed! [Editor's note]

able and determined minority sufficed to thwart a project, or even that unanimity was required for a decision. In most parliaments, indeed, the principle of majority rule was sooner or later established. But there are numerous examples to show the long survival or the reappearance of the older ideas.

For taxes, at least, unanimous agreement was necessary, so it was claimed in Castile, in the German Reichstag, in the Papal States. In the Dutch Republic unanimity was required for decisions of the States-General about taxes, peace or war, and for decisions of the Provincial Estates about a large and indefinite number of questions. In the Swiss Federal Diet almost all matters could be settled only by unanimous vote. In Hungary a statute of 1495 provided that a question on which parliament divided was to be settled *per sententiam sanioris partis: i. e.,* by the opinion, not necessarily of the majority, but, as it was interpreted, "of the wiser and more powerful part of the nation." In the Russian *Zemski Sobors* the majority principle seems never to have been established. In Catalonia, where majority rule did prevail among clergy and cities, unanimity was required in the noble estate, so that a single nobleman could thwart a project by declaring, *Yo dissent.* In Valencia all decisions, to be valid, must be passed by the noblesse *nemine discrepante* — hence the pleasant tale of a certain incorrigible minority of one which could be overcome only by throwing "the idiot" into the street. In Aragon unanimous agreement was demanded not only in one estate, but in all four; and any member could defeat a proposal merely by uttering the word, *Disiento.* Old writers jested that any law or act of the Cortes in Aragon was a miracle. But the acme of exaggerated individualism was reached in Poland with the famous Liberum Veto, through which, as practiced from 1652 on, a single member of the Diet, by the simple formula, *Nie pozwalam* ("I will not permit"), could not only thwart the proposal to which he objected, but also

dissolve the Diet at once and nullify all the decisions previously made by the assembly.

Another bane of medieval parliaments was the system of imperative mandates. A deputy, being considered as an ambassador or procurator more than as a national counsellor, usually received from his constituents more or less detailed instructions, which often limited and hampered him in the extreme. If the matters to come up in parliament were known in advance, he might have the line that he was to follow absolutely prescribed: if not, he might be ordered to agree to nothing without consulting his constituents. Still further to increase his sense of responsibility, he might be required, at the close of parliament, to give a full account of his conduct at a special meeting of the local assembly that had elected him (as in the "relation" dietines or congregations of Poland, Hungary, and East Prussia). Severe punishments might threaten one who overstepped his mandate: in Switzerland, for instance, more than one deputy paid with his head for so doing.

While practice varied greatly in different countries and at different periods, in general it may be said that more or less imperative mandates were widely used in almost every parliament of the period, except in England and Aragon. Although the system had its merits in strengthening the hands of the estates against the crown, it was on the whole disastrous, particularly because of the endless delays resulting from it, and because it tended to the settlement of national questions on the basis of narrow local views and interests. Especially in certain countries like Castile, France, Germany, Poland, and Hungary, this was one of the worst obstacles to the efficient functioning of the national assembly.

Parliamentary technique, though in general still crude, does show various interesting developments in that period. One was the extensive use of committees. Often they were employed during the sessions of the assembly to effect an agreement between the estates or with the crown; to draft responses, petitions, or legislation; to handle special matters, such as those that required secrecy, or judicial business. Some parliaments came near to abdicating their functions into the hands of a committee. In Naples, for instance, in the sixteenth and seventeenth centuries, the *Parlamento-Generale* did little save to vote the subsidies and then elect a committee called the *Parlamento-Senato,* which attended to nearly all other business. Still more omnipotent was the famous committee in Scotland called the "Lords of the Articles," which from the later fourteenth to the seventeenth century almost replaced the national assembly, at times even legislating and levying taxes quite independently. As late as the reign of Charles I, the Scots Parliament was wont to meet only twice in a session: the first time to choose the Lords of the Articles, and the second time to go through the form of sanctioning what they had done. And in various German states in the later period full meetings of the Diet virtually ceased to be held, being replaced by committees of the estates (*Ausschusstage*). Finally, one may note the custom of electing a committee which, during the intervals between parliamentary sessions, was to watch over the liberties of the estates, or the execution of decisions or laws made in parliament, or to carry on various political, administrative, or financial tasks that parliament had assumed. In the eastern Spanish kingdoms, in certain French provinces like Languedoc or Brittany, in Naples and Sicily, and in nearly all the German states these standing committees ("Deputations," "*Ausschüsse*") became one of the most important elements in the political life of the country, largely making up for infrequent or irregular meetings of parliament and subjecting the crown to a considerable measure of supervision and control.

Medieval assemblies usually ended, as they began, with a joint session of all the estates in the presence of the prince or his representatives. In some lands like France or Castile, these final sessions were likely to be perfunctory and meaningless, the king, after wringing taxes out of the deputies, being chiefly anxious to send them home at once without listening to their grievances. But in many countries the final session had the utmost importance. It was then and then alone that parliament effectually transacted business. For the custom had arisen that none of the agreements previously reached during the assembly should be regarded as definitive until at the end all of them — the concessions [made by the estates to the crown and the concessions] made by the crown to the estates — were gathered up into one great final act, which, after being solemnly sanctioned by crown and estates alike at the final session, acquired binding force. This system of "final acts," "articles," "capitulations," "recesses," or whatsoever they might be called, is found in Scotland, Aragon, Catalonia, Valencia, Sicily, all the German Diets, Sweden, Bohemia, Hungary, and Poland. As a technical device for binding the crown and making the grant of taxes dependent upon the redress of grievances, it was admirable; but its disadvantages are obvious, particularly the fact that if a parliament broke up without coming to a "final act," all the previous work of the session went for nothing. At any rate, such compacts between crown and estates, almost like treaties between independent sovereigns, illustrate the dualistic conception of the state that underlies the parliamentarism of this period in its more developed forms.

The competence of these assemblies can seldom be defined with any accuracy, for it was bounded by no systematic constitutions of the modern sort. The estates almost everywhere did, indeed, at one time or another wring from their rulers written recognition of their rights in this or that respect; and, apart from this, the unwritten law of customs and precedents generally established for them a certain more or less incontestable sphere of activity. But at bottom everything depended on the ever-varying political situation and the ever-shifting balance of power as between the crown and the estates. Whenever the crown felt strong enough, it was prone to forget, to deny, or to ride roughshod over inconvenient parliamentary rights, no matter whether they were based on custom or on sacred charters. And when the prince was weak, or a minor, or badly in debt, or the land in a great crisis, the estates in their turn were likely to take the bit in their teeth, to extend their scope almost without limits, or even virtually to sequestrate the government. When the crown was up, parliament was down, and vice versa — that is the most general rule that can be laid down in the matter.

The most constant and important activity of the estates was the granting of taxes. *Landtage sind Geldtage* — that German adage might have been applied to nearly all these parliaments. Almost everywhere (save in Russia, Denmark, and Norway), the principle came to be recognized that, apart from the old feudal and domain revenues, no taxes could be imposed without the consent of the estates. It was by exploiting the power of the purse that not only the English Parliament but many Continental ones raised themselves to a high degree of power and indispensability. And it may be said that in most countries the sole right of the estates to grant taxes was, on the whole, well maintained down to the seventeenth century. There is, however, the well-known exception of France, where the States-General lost this power from 1440 on, and the Provincial Estates, from about the same period, could do little more than debate how taxes that could not be escaped might best be paid.

The second chief sphere of parliamentary activity was in legislation. All these assemblies had at least some influence in this field, through their right to present petitions and grievances (*cahiers de doléances, greujes, agravís, postulata, gravamina*), which even in countries like France furnished the stimulus and the material for a great deal of royal law-making. The French States-General and the Castilian and Portuguese Cortes in the later period scarcely got beyond this. But nothing could be more erroneous than the assumption often made (by writers whose knowledge of Continental systems hardly extends beyond France or Castile) that the English Parliament was the only assembly of that time that discovered how to gain effective legislative power by making grants of supply depend on redress of grievances, and by drawing up their demands in the form of "bills" ready to become "acts" as soon as they received the royal sanction. In fact both these devices came to be practiced in most Continental parliaments: in the eastern Spanish kingdoms, Sicily, the German states, Sweden, Poland, Bohemia, and Hungary. Usually this did not exclude a certain amount of legislation by the crown without the sanction of the estates; but, on the other hand, in Germany at least within certain spheres the estates could legislate without the sanction of the crown. In general, the principle was widespread that all more important laws ought to be made only with the consent and participation of parliament; and there were kingdoms like Poland or Aragon where this principle was very strictly carried out.

Thirdly, there was a vast range of functions which most parliaments sometimes arrogated to themselves, especially in times of crisis and confusion, and some of which were exercised for long periods by some of these assemblies. Foreign relations were a matter in which most estates often claimed a voice. They wished to be consulted about war, peace, alliances, treaties; nay, sometimes they sent and received embassies, raised armies, and concluded peace or alliances quite of their own authority. Similarly, the history of most parliaments shows attempts to dictate the choice of the prince's advisers or to force upon him a council formally elected by the estates (which the Swedish kings had to submit to through much of the eighteenth century). There are many cases of a parliament appointing a regent, fixing the succession to the throne, or even for long periods freely electing its rulers. Even more common was the custom that the estates should prescribe how the taxes they granted should be expended, or should undertake the collection and disbursement through their own agents and treasury. Many parliaments (e. g., the eastern Spanish kingdoms, Languedoc, Brittany, the German states) came to have quite a staff of permanent officials of their own, and to take a large part not only in the financial but in the general administration of the country. Finally, the assumption sometimes made that the English Parliament alone combined the functions of a legislative and tax-granting body with those of a high court of justice is by no means true: many Continental assemblies of estates present the same combination of functions (e. g., in Aragon, Poland, and universally among the German states).

It is also a mistake, and a not uncommon one, to suppose that all the Continental estates died premature deaths as in France, and that England alone kept her parliament continuously down to modern times. It is true that the seventeenth and early eighteenth centuries saw the extinction of not a few of the old parliaments. They disappear in most of the French provinces (under Richelieu and Louis XIV), in Portugal (after 1697), the eastern Spanish kingdoms (1707–14), Naples (after 1634), Piedmont (after 1582), Savoy (after 1766), in some of the German territories, like Bavaria (after 1669), in Denmark and Norway (after 1661), in Russia (after 1682). But they survived down to the French Revolution in many instances: in a dozen French provinces, in Castile, Navarre, Sicily, the Dutch Republic, Belgium, the German Imperial Diet, many German states (like Saxony and Hanover), Austria, Bohemia, Hungary, Poland, and Sweden. In most of these cases, indeed, the hand of the monarch was heavy upon them, and the estates seemed sunk in lethargy or stricken with palsy. But

in some instances — notably in Sweden, Poland, Hungary, and among the German states especially in Württemberg — the old parliaments continued to show a great deal of life and activity down to the end.

The assemblies that have been surveyed here had many defects and weaknesses. They were not, at least for modern times, sufficiently representative: they rested on too narrow a class basis. In their later, decadent period they generally tended to identify themselves too much with antiquated political and social ideals, and with selfish class and local interests. In most cases the crown prevailed over them because it, better than they, represented the trend towards national unity, social equality, and efficient government. These parliaments suffered equally from the lack of solidarity and coöperation among the several social classes: from those jealousies and conflicts between the estates which played such a rôle in France in 1789, or which enabled the Danish crown in 1660 by a *coup d'état* to make itself absolute. And there are many other weaknesses that might be listed: the chaotic methods of electing deputies, imperative mandates, the multiplicity of chambers, the difficulty of enforcing the will of the majority, the unpopularity which in many countries always clung to these assemblies because they were associated in men's minds only with new taxes, the desire so often manifested even by the privileged classes to escape from participating in parliament in order to avoid an ungrateful task and onerous responsibilities.

Nevertheless, the old parliaments in many ways rendered important services. They gave the crown what was on the whole, a fruitful and a long indispensable coöperation in building up, out of the chaos and disintegration of feudalism, the unified modern state. By drawing representatives of the leading social classes and of every locality together into regular collaboration on common problems, they helped much to create a sense of common interests and a national spirit. We may also be grateful to them for having through centuries implanted and maintained in most European countries certain precious ideas about constitutional liberty, the rights of peoples as against monarchs, no taxation without representation, government carried on through and with the consent of the governed, the representative system. Those ideas might be for a time obscured, but they were never lost. And when in the nineteenth century the new movements for democracy and constitutionalism set in, most European nations did not need to look abroad entirely for guidance: nearly everywhere the friends of liberty could find traditions, precedents, principles, and inspiration in the records of their own parliaments of the Middle Ages.

THE LIMITATIONS OF ABSOLUTISM IN THE "NEW MONARCHIES"

J. RUSSELL MAJOR

THE concept of a renaissance has been defended and attacked ever since Burckhardt published his *Civilization of the Renaissance* in Italy nearly a century ago. There are those who see in the fifteenth and sixteenth centuries a definite period of European history. Others recognize in these years only a continued growth that had begun well back in the Middle Ages. Still others look on the two centuries as witnessing the decline of the medieval civilization. The attitude of the scholar is determined in part by his field of research. The art historian, for example, is usually a strong supporter of the thesis that there was a Renaissance and that it constituted a definite historical period. The economic historian often prefers to see the real change as taking place around the eleventh century with the revival of trade and the growth of towns. The devout Catholic, on the other hand, interprets the period as being one of a decline beginning with the false teachings of William of Occam and ending in the horrible tragedy of Luther and Descartes. Students of literature, science, philosophy, and political theory have added their ideas to further confuse the concept of the Renaissance; but although there are political histories aplenty, little effort has been made to interpret the period from the standpoint of the nature of the state, this in spite of the fact that Burckhardt saw in the peculiar political situation in Italy one of the principal causes of the Italian Renaissance.

The purpose of this paper is to explore the nature of monarchies to the north and west of Italy, paying particular attention to France. It is my hope to add support to Burckhardt's thesis that the state of this period differed enough from what had gone before and what was to come after, to constitute a definite period in history, but to deny that the Swiss scholar's bold characterization of the Renaissance city-state as being a work of art, that is, "the fruit of reflection and careful adaptation," has any validity for the monarchies at that time.

In developing the concept of a Renaissance Monarchy for France, we miss the

From J. Russell Major, "'The Renaissance Monarchy: A Contribution to the Periodization of History," *Emory University Quarterly* (1957), pp. 112–124. Reprinted by permission of the author and the *Emory University Quarterly*.

dynastic changes that make such convenient, though not entirely accurate, marks of delineation for England, yet it seems undeniable that there was considerable difference between the monarchies of, let us say, Philip IV, Francis I, and Louis XIV, between the Medieval, the Renaissance, and the Baroque. The system of government typified by Francis I had its formative period during the reigns of Charles VII and Louis XI and its period of decline during the reigns of Henry IV and Louis XIII.

The first and most pronounced characteristic of this monarchy was its dynastic structure and motivation. Foreign and domestic policy centered around the question of marriages, for it was by marriages that states were enlarged. Wars of conquest were undertaken to secure a claimed inheritance not natural boundaries. The national and economic considerations that loom so large in modern statecraft were ignored, and we find Charles VIII surrendering land in what is now southern France to Spain and what is now northern France to the Habsburgs in order to buy their neutrality before he embarked on an expedition to conquer Naples, for which he had a dynastic claim. Not until the reign of Louis XIV did the French kings abandon their desire to win Italy and adopt as their goal the achievement of their stategic boundaries of the Pyrenees and the Rhine. Before one condemns this type of diplomacy, however, it should be remembered that it was by marriage that the Habsburgs built the mighty empire of Charles V. His lands were more extensive than those of Napoleon or Hitler and his empire was to endure far longer.

Internal policy also depended largely on marriage. Nobles were sometimes able to amass enough land to become threats to one or even two monarchs. The Burgundian dukes brought together so many duchies and counties in France and the Empire that they posed a serious problem to both the Valois and the Emperor. The House of Foix-Navarre won huge estates on both sides of the Pyrenees. Other families did likewise, but if a noble house could build its power by dynastic arrangements, the kings could profit by the extinction of a great family, for when there was no heir, feudal territories escheated back to the crown. It was by this process that the French monarchy added so much to its domain, and a large part of the internal policy of the Valois was designed to further the work of nature and chance. Louis XI married his crippled daughter, who could have no children, to the Duke of Orléans in order to insure the eventual acquisition of his lands, while two French kings sought and won the hand of Anne of Brittany to keep her highly prized duchy united with the crown.

Since territorial aggrandizement at the expense of foreign states and the local nobility depended on dynastic claims and feudal law, legality had to be stressed to an unusual degree. The Renaissance prince has often been pictured as a highly individualistic ruler with little respect for aught save wit and power, but in fact even the Italian potentate was ever anxious to find legal justification for the authority he wielded, and elsewhere rulers were still less subject to challenge on this score.

This stress on legitimacy and legality by the Renaissance Monarchs was not limited to their own rights, it involved a respect for the rights of their subjects. When a new king came to the throne, he invariably confirmed the privileges of individuals, towns, provinces, and other corporate groups in his kingdom. When a princely or feudal domain fell to a king, he at once recognized the privileges its inhabitants had been granted by their previous rulers. Indeed, the people of the newly incorporated territories were as apt to accept the orders of their new sovereign by virtue of his being Count of Provence or Duke of Brittany as King of France.

The acceptance of the idea of legitimacy and privilege and the existence of strong provincial loyalties made necessary a decentralized form of government. Not only were the customs, laws, and privileges of each and every territory recognized, but the kings established sovereign law courts in the larger provinces. Thus *Parlements* or courts of justice, and several types of financial courts were organized in Burgundy, Languedoc, Brittany, Provence, Dauphiné, and elsewhere from which there was no appeal to any higher court at Paris. The decisions of these courts were based on law, custom, and tradition, and not until the mid-seventeenth century is there evidence that any universal principles of reason and morality were applied. The judges could and did render decisions against royal officials and the crown itself, although the king, as the fountain of justice, was able to overrule their objections by a personal appearance. The existence of these courts provided assurance that the three hundred odd local customs in France would be preserved until the Revolution.

The legal decentralization described above was paralleled by the decentralization of administration. There was a governor in each of the dozen or more great provinces of France who, with or without royal approval, assumed the various regalian powers. In addition, about two-thirds of the provinces had representative assemblies that voted, and often collected taxes and attended to other administrative matters. Beneath the provinces were the bailiwicks and seneschalries. These jurisdictions were ruled by the bailiff or seneschal and a host of lesser officials who, like the governors, were as apt to follow their own desires as to obey the directives of the king.

Alongside the hierarchy of the royal officials there existed the seigneury and the town. The seigneurs were still a power in the villages, and it has often been pointed out that the peasant rarely came into contact with royal authority except to pay taxes. The towns were largely self-governing, with their own elected officials, independent systems of taxation, and militia to defend their fortified walls. Thus, the land the kings won by their dynastic policies did not point to a consolidation of power in the hands of the central government as much as to the acceptance of the diversified, decentralized conglomeration of provinces, duchies, counties, seigneuries, and towns that was the Renaissance Monarchy.

Closely associated with the decentralization of the Renaissance Monarchy was the confusion of boundaries, privileges, rights, and jurisdictions only too apparent in every branch of the government. The sea provided the only clearly defined boundary of the Renaissance state. Elsewhere much land was in dispute. Territories, independent, or with strong claim to independence, such as the duchy of Bouillon, the principalities of Montbéliard, Bidache, and Salm, the republics of Mandure and Mulhouse, the counties of Sarrverden, Venaissin, and Sault, to say nothing of the papal state of Avignon and the principality of Orange existed along the borders and even in the interior of the country. Many of these enclaves owned smaller enclaves in France, while France, in turn, was sometimes in possession of parishes surrounded by these enclaves. There is ample evidence to show that often neither the French king, the foreign ruler, nor the local magistrates could agree on what they owned. Foreigners held fiefs in France, and in the bailiwick of Gex they sought to vote in the elections to the Estates General of 1789. Ecclesiastical boundaries rarely coincided with those of the nation and the dioceses of many foreign archbishops and bishops included parishes in France. Two of these foreign prelates were actually elected deputies to the Estates General in 1789.

More serious was the confusion about the boundaries of the administrative subdivisions of the kingdom. Nearly every bailiwick had jurisdiction over parishes completely surrounded by neighboring bailiwicks. Frequently parishes and even towns were claimed by rival royal authorities. It was impossible for any magistrate to know exactly what territory he was to administer. As late as 1789 there were no less than 1800 divided or contested parishes in France. Many secondary bailiwicks claimed independence from the principal bailiwick to which they had been traditionally considered to be attached. There were quarrels about the extent and nature of the justice in countless seigneuries. Each town possessed its special privileges, which more often than not differed from those of its neighbor. Royal officials sometimes had only the vaguest idea of the rights of each. The resultant confusion was so great that it was difficult for officials to govern or the law to operate. Disobedience could safely become commonplace, and one is not surprised to find one aristocrat writing after the Revolution that before 1789 people enjoyed "the most complete liberty. One was free to speak, to write, to act with the greatest independence, and one could even defy the authorities in perfect security." Certainly Burckhardt's description of the Italian city-state as being "the fruit of reflection and careful adaptation" has no validity for the monarchies of that time.

Why did the Renaissance Monarchs of France and other countries permit so much decentralization and confusion? Why did they respect the privileges of their subjects? The answer to these questions lies partly in the fact that the rulers were products of the climate of opinion of their age. They had been taught that a king was responsible for the well-being of his subjects, that to deprive them of their long-recognized privileges was to become a tyrant, and tyranny was as hateful in their age as it had been in the medieval period. Nowhere does this fact show more clearly than in the decisions rendered by the king in council. These invaluable records provide the most trustworthy evidence we have for the motives behind the actions of the kings and their principal advisors. They prove that the crown had even greater respect for privilege and tradition than the regular law courts, and give direct contradiction to any theory that the Renaissance Monarchs sought to increase their authority at the expense of the legitimate rights of their subjects. Indeed, the most frequent type of dispute to be brought before the council resulted from the encroachments of local royal officials in the name of the king on the prerogatives and privileges of individuals and corporate groups, but almost invariably the decision of the councillors favored the privileged to the discomfiture of the over-zealous local officials. There was, of course, the possibility that a ruler would recklessly break the bonds of tradition or that he would be so self-righteous as to interpret every questionable royal prerogative in his own favor; but if there were such kings, their weakness in character was checkmated by their weakness in power.

It has been generally assumed that the establishment of standing armies on the continent in the late fifteenth and sixteenth centuries furthered the growth of royal absolutism. However, the most casual examination of the size and composition of the new armies dispels any illusion of their being an effective instrument against the people. The troops in the peacetime army and militia of France seldom numbered more than one and a half modern divisions. Even with the rapid transportation and communication of today coupled with the immense superiority of the arms and training of the modern soldier over the civilian population, such a force could hardly subject an unwilling population of fifteen million persons. Witness the recent difficulties of the Russians in Hungary. Furthermore, the system of livery and maintenance or clientage gave the great noble a military force of his own. The Duke of Montmorency came to court in 1560 with a retinue of 800 horsemen, and he could have mustered a larger force had there been any need. Fortified towns the size of Troyes and Amiens had 3000 militiamen equipped with artillery and munitions. Thus, while the king could have captured the castles of a Montmorency and taken any single town in the kingdom, it was cheaper and easier for a ruler to avoid offending his subjects, and any sort of an attack on the privileges of the nobility or towns as a whole was clearly impossible.

It is true that in time of war the Renaissance Monarchs sometimes had armies of 40,000 or 50,000 men, but these troops were raised and paid by their officers, and not the state. They therefore obeyed their commanders and not the king. As late as the Thirty Years War both the French king and the Emperor were often more endangered by their own disobedient troops than by the troops of the enemy. Some of these forces were officered by mercenaries, but the bulk were commanded by the native nobility, who could hardly be expected to turn on their fellow nobles or even the towns on the directives of the king.

If the Renaissance Monarchs lacked the military power to suppress their subjects, they also lacked the bureaucracy to govern them. In 1505 there were only 12,000 royal officials in France, a nation of 15,000,-000 inhabitants and 480,000 square kilometers, or one official for each 1,250 inhabitants and one for each 40 square kilometers. In 1934 there was one official for each 70 inhabitants and 56 for each 40 square kilometers. Furthermore, it was impossible for the Renaissance Monarch to control the limited number of officials he possessed. In the first place, whereas the Washington bureaucrat is armed with a typewriter, a mimeograph machine, the government printing office, and rapid means of communication, the Renaissance Monarch had only a limited number of scribes to record his orders. When he wanted to send a directive to the bailiffs, he had to have it copied by hand a hundred times, for there were a hundred bailiffs. As a result, orders from the central government were few and brief, leaving local officials very much to their own devices. The printing press was, of course, known, but as late as 1600 it was used only to print important ordonnances, and not for normal administrative correspondence.

In the second place, the financial difficulties that beset the Renaissance Monarchs led them to sell government posts, and once an office became venal, its holder could not normally be discharged without financial reimbursement. He was left free to obey or disobey the few brief directives he received with little likelihood that the king would ever know the difference, or that if he did, he could do anything about it.

If, then, the Renaissance kings lacked a strong, loyal army and an adequate obedient bureaucracy, what was the basis of monarchical power? The answer seems clear. Kings were obeyed only because, or rather when, the bulk of the population supported their cause. The devotion of the French people to their king was described by a Venetian ambassador as "a unique thing in the Christian world." The purpose of Machiavelli's *The Prince* was to teach how power could be won and maintained, and no one was more certain than the author that it was more important for a ruler of his day to satisfy the people than the military, because "the people are the more powerful." To secure the support of the people, the prince was advised to appear to have all the traditional virtues, to tax lightly, and when great feudal dependencies were won back, to alter neither the laws nor the taxes of the inhabitants. The more experienced Commynes likewise advised kings to secure the affection of their subjects. Even Cardinal Richelieu wrote that "love is the most powerful motive which obliges one to obey."

The Renaissance kings were supported by their subjects for a number of reasons. They were the restorers of order after a long period of warfare marked by all the horrors of pillaging and murdering by undisciplined soldiers. There was no safe, logical alternative to their rule, however much town and noble might be opposed to further increases in royal power. They accurately sensed the feelings of the people and, as we have seen, were ever ready to support and protect their privileges even against their own officials. They kept in intimate contact with the people by wandering from one part of their kingdom to another, receiving everyone without barriers of rigid formality. Indeed, there was a degree of intimacy between the kings and their people that surprised the ambassadors of republican Venice. In 1561 one of them attributed the devotion of the French people to the crown to "the familiarity which exists between the monarch and his subjects all of whom he treats as his companions. No one is excluded from his presence. Lackeys and people of lowest condition dare to enter the private office of the king in order to see everything that happens and to hear all that is said. If one wishes to speak of something important, he must have the patience to find a place where there are not a great many people and then speak in a low voice in order not to be heard. This great familiarity, it is true, makes the subjects insolent, but at the same time it makes them faithful and devoted to their kings." We would do well to picture the Renaissance Monarch as being the "first gentleman" of France rather than the "Sun King." The removal of the court to Versailles by Louis XIV was symbolic of the separation of the crown from the people during his reign, and the return of the court to Paris in 1789 could have had equal importance had an abler man been the head of the state.

A more tangible way of winning support also lay in the power of the kings. They controlled a vast system of patronage. Most of the highest offices of the church lay at their disposal and the wealthiest bishoprics and abbeys went to their faithful supporters. Government positions, one of the most lucrative of all forms of employment during the period, found their way into the same hands. Fiefs, patents of nobility, and nearly every type of privilege could be granted by the monarch. He who served the crown loyally and ably could hope for untold riches. Montmorency, Wolsey, and Richelieu were only the most famous of those who won wealth and power through loyalty. Thousands of lesser names could be added.

One last way of winning popular support was through the use of representative institutions. It may seem strange that kings encouraged and developed assemblies of the estates, but since neither the medieval nor the Renaissance Monarchs had ever heard of representative government, they could have foreseen no reason to fear or destroy representative assemblies. They regarded these institutions as tools for their use, like their councils and their judicial and financial courts. It is true that representative assemblies sometimes got out of hand, but did not the council also check the king upon occasion? As long as no one thought that either the council or the assembly could govern alone, the one was no more dangerous than the other, and both could prove of value upon occasion. The uses of the estates were discovered during the Middle Ages, and strong monarchs, as Edward I of England and Philip IV of France, did not hesitate to summon large assemblies.

The practice of holding national assemblies declined in most countries in the fourteenth century, but was revived by the Renaissance Monarchs. These kings were faced with problems growing out of two great changes. One was the influx of precious metals from the New World which led to a rapid rise in prices. Higher prices, in turn, necessitated higher taxes and led to social unrest. The second great change was the Protestant Revolt. Sooner or later nearly every European dynasty had to deal with a rebellious religious minority. The kings had neither the bureaucracy nor the army to cope with the new situation. Their only hope was to win the support of the people for whatever action they determined to take. This they could best do by summoning the deputies of the people and explaining to them their policy and needs. It was not often that the burgher from the town or the seigneur from the manor mustered sufficient courage to resist the crown on these occasions, and once a Parliament or Estates General had committed itself to the desired course, the king had a powerful propaganda weapon. He could claim that he had won the sanction of the people in the ordonnance he issued, and in the deputies he had valuable agents who explained the royal policy to their constituents when they returned to their homes.

The kings had no fear of the assemblies of the estates because these institutions were generally not considered to have any independent power. Indeed, the prevailing argument, perhaps put forth by the kings themselves, was that representative assemblies served to increase royal power by enabling them to extend their influence into fields of activity ordinarily denied to them. This attitude is illustrated by Philippe de Commynes when, in writing of a proposed invasion of the continent in 1474 by England, he said: "But things move very slowly there because the king cannot undertake such work without assembling his parliament, which is like our three estates, and, consisting of sober and pious men, is very serviceable and a great strengthening to the king. When these estates are assembled, he declares his intention and asks his subjects for an aid."

To Commynes the English Parliament did not decrease the power of the king by preventing him from levying an aid without consent. Rather Parliament increased his power by making it possible for him legally to obtain money beyond his ordinary revenue. In the same spirit Henry VIII declared to the Commons in 1543: "We at no time stand so highly in our estate royal as in time of Parliament, wherein we as head and you as members are conjoined and knit together in one body politic."

Henry III of France stated that "holding the estates is a means . . . to reaffirm the legitimate authority of the sovereign rather than to disturb or diminish it." Jean Bodin wrote: "We conclude, therefore, that the sovereignty of the monarch is neither altered nor diminished by the presence of the estates. On the contrary, his majesty is much greater and more illustrious seeing his people acknowledge him as their sovereign."

Statements such as these could be multiplied without end, and nearly all the Renaissance Monarchs put theory into practice by endeavoring to use representative institutions as a means of winning popular support for their program. In every country from Spain to Sweden rulers turned to their representative institutions for additional taxes, and in England, Denmark, and Sweden the kings successfully used their estates or Parliaments to introduce Protestantism. In the Empire, Scotland, the Low Countries, and France the monarchs also went to the estates to solve the religious problem, but with less success. Civil wars broke out, and it was only then that the theory began to develop that the representative institution had an authority separate from the crown. It was only then that the kings began to dread the meetings of the estates.

I have described the Renaissance Monarchy as being a decentralized state with confused boundaries and jurisdictions, but motivated by the forces of dynasticism, legality, and tradition. Its strength lay not in the size or loyalty of its army or bureaucracy, but rather in the support it received from the people. It remains to be shown that the nature of this state differed enough from what had gone before and what was to come after to give support to the thesis that the Renaissance constitutes a separate period in history.

The medieval state had also been dynastic, traditional, decentralized, and confused. It had relied on popular support, but it nevertheless differed from that of the Renaissance. Medieval decentralization was derived largely from the activities of the great feudal nobles and their vassals. Renaissance decentralization was essentially bureaucratic. Thus in the Middle Ages the duchy of Burgundy was governed by her duke, in the Renaissance it was ruled by a royal governor and subordinate officials; there were several types of sovereign courts to administer justice and provincial estates to negotiate with the crown. It was not the individual rights of the Duke of Burgundy that were stressed in regard to the crown, but rather the collective privileges of the inhabitants of the duchy.

A combination of time and degree also separates the medieval from the Renaissance. The thirteenth-century monarchs had been strong, those of the fourteenth and early fifteenth centuries were weak, but the kings of the sixteenth century were again men of ability. A Henry VI provides a break in the continuity between Edward I and Henry VIII. Furthermore, the Renaissance Monarchs were able to do bigger things. The medieval king helped open trade in the Mediterranean; the Renaissance king aided in the discovery of the water route to India and the New World. The medieval king encouraged an economic revival characterized by merchant and craft guilds, the Renaissance king sparked a commercial and industrial revolution. The former exercised a minor influence in arts and letters, the latter were the greatest patrons of their age.

The break between the Renaissance Monarchy and that of the late seventeenth and eighteenth centuries is more pronounced. Dynastic politics did not completely disappear, but national and economic considerations became more important. Armies became larger and the kings won effective control over them. Commanders in the wars of Louis XIV did not change sides at will as they had done during the Thirty Years War. The bureaucracies became larger and more efficient. The intendant of Louis XIV and the carefully trained officials of the Great Elector of Brandenburg were only the finest examples of what was a general European phenomenon. The popular-consultative aspects of the Renaissance Monarchy were abandoned. Kings ceased to wander from place to place, but preferred to remain in one or two favorite palaces. Elaborate court etiquette shut them off from all but their most favorite subjects. The official press replaced the representative assembly as the means to control public opinion. It is no coincidence that the reign of Louis XIII saw the last meeting of the Estates General until the Revolution, and the appearance of a government-controlled newspaper and an official annual news journal. Gradually the rational and ordered conceptions of the seventeenth century with the preference for the simple over the complex permeated governments. Judicial decisions came to be rendered in the name of the universal principles of justice rather than being based on custom alone. The decentralized conglomerations of duchies and counties so characteristic of the Renaissance Monarchy became abhorrent, and officials consciously sought to weld them into the centralized, well-ordered state. The new approach was clearly expressed by a minister of Philip IV of Spain when he said: "The most important task that confronts your Majesty is to make yourself King of Spain; by which I mean, Sir, that your Majesty should not rest content with the titles of King of Portugal, King of Aragon, King of Valencia, and Count of Barcelona, but that your majesty should labor and plan, with careful and secret consideration, to reduce all these realms of which Spain is now composed, to the fashion and laws of Castile, without any difference." When a royal advisor could make this statement, the state had indeed become "the fruit of reflection and careful adaptation." Our modern age had finally been born.

POLLARD'S "NEW MONARCHY":
THE NEGATION OF ORTHODOXY

J. H. HEXTER

Professor Hexter was born in 1910. He took a Ph.D. at Harvard during the Great Depression, a fact which he relates to his own failure to produce "magisterial works." Be that as it may, he has devoted his talents to pelting historians à la mode with the missiles fashioned by his sharp wit and trenchant criticism. His works, including *King Pym* and *Utopia; Biography of an Idea,* established him as a leading critic of historically orthodox views. Numerous articles, including the present selection originally entitled "Factors in Modern History," were gathered together in 1961 as *Reappraisals in History: New Views on History and Society in Early Modern Europe.* In his own words, he has devoted himself to stating a "negation of an orthodoxy" — in this case the views of A. F. Pollard.

To allay any perplexity that may have assailed the reader on a hasty reading of the title of this essay, it may be well to point out that that title is not *Factors in Modern History* but *quote Factors in Modern History close-quote,* and that the operative signs are the quotation marks. In this essay, therefore, there will be no effort, doomed to futility at the outset, to deal in a few pages with the factors — whatever they may be — in modern history — whatever that is. This paper is about no such vast subject, but about a rather short book called *Factors in Modern History.* The book was published over half a century ago, in 1907; and its author was Professor A. F. Pollard.

Pollard was a great academic statesman — not an academic who made his way in national politics, but an imaginative builder within the bounds of Academe. Among the historians of his day in England no other left as a legacy so many active and lively institutions for the advancement of historical knowledge. Indeed, if the creation and fostering of such institutions is the best measure of academic statesmanship, then Pollard not only towers above his contemporaries among the historians, but must stand near the top among all the men of learning of his day both in England and elsewhere. As early as 1903 he had envisioned the complex structure of interlacing groups and activities that were needed to make a great history school at the University of London; and what he had envisioned he had the good fortune, the vigor, the courage and the tenacity to bring into being long before he died. The Historical Association, the journal *History,* the Institute of Historical Research, and the *Bulletin* of that Institute are more than inert monuments to Pollard's energy and effectiveness, and they do more than serve as passive memorials of their spiritual father. Rather they continue his creativity by carrying on in their independent existences the work he had nearest his heart.

Professor Pollard was also a notable scholar. There are not many historical

From J. H. Hexter, *Reappraisals in History; New Views on History and Society in Early Modern Europe* (New York and London, 1961), pp. 26–44. Reprinted by permission of Northwestern University Press and Longmans, Green and Company Ltd.

surveys of which, fifty years after their publication, one can say they are still the best things available. But one can say just that of Pollard's volume on the history of England from 1547 to 1603. And of course his biographies of Henry VIII, Cranmer, and Wolsey remain without peer.

Factors in Modern History was no such peerless performance, and certainly Pollard would not have claimed that it was so. Why then, a reader might properly ask, should he have inflicted on him a long disquisition on a book written more than half a century ago, a book which, although it possesses a certain excellence, can hardly be described as a classic of history? One might answer that, classic or not, *Factors in Modern History* is still quite a live book. In America within the past year it has been freed from larval compression between hard covers and metamorphosed, indeed apotheosized, into a paper-back. Moreover, so it has been told me, generations of English schoolmasters have used *Factors in Modern History* to introduce sixth formers to the study of history above the merely infantile level. It has thus become a bit of standard equipment for the initiation rites of the historical phratry.

Yet even were it less gorgeously covered with badges of success, the book would warrant close examination. For the purpose of this study *Factors in Modern History* has a special virtue which results from the quality of A. F. Pollard's mind. It was a mind strong and shrewd, but neither particularly sensitive nor particularly subtle. In *Factors in Modern History* that mind produced a work of broad generalization. The book portrays in primary hues and with little reserve or qualification the best thought of fifty years ago — a good part of it Pollard's own — on the seventeenth century and on that particularly difficult period, the sixteenth century. One would have said the Tudor period, were it not that in this book Pollard casts his glance, somewhat casually and dimly one must confess, at continental Europe. *Factors in Modern History*, therefore, provides us with a sort of color chart. Contrasting it with the views of present-day historians on the sixteenth and seventeenth century, we become aware of some of the changes that have taken place in our understanding of history in the past fifty years.

Before we make such a contrast, however, we ought to render to Pollard the homage that is his due for the assault he made on certain historical idols of his own day. It was a day — before Armageddon — when English liberal Parliamentary democracy was riding high, and when its supposed excellences were frequently ascribed to certain superior national traits putatively inherent in the English race. On the kind of historical thinking that produced pronouncements — solemn, pompous and silly — on the role of race in English history, Pollard wrought a splendid destruction. And of history writing that praised a mythical Lancastrian constitution because it was supposed to have advanced toward Parliamentary supremacy, and damned the Tudors because they were supposed to have inhibited the growth of Parliament, he made short work. If it did not make it impossible for historians to talk such nonsense — nothing seems to prevent a really determined historian from talking nonsense — at least the publication of *Factors in Modern History* made it more difficult, and demanded of the historian a more headlong propensity toward fatuousness. For his holocaust of historical idols we are all still debtors to A. F. Pollard.

Now, having rendered our meed of praise, we must turn to the less congenial, but more essential, task of exploring the deficiencies that the past half-century of historical study has revealed in Pollard's work. In so doing, we in no way belittle the man or his work. He and, with far less skill, we, work in the same craft, the art of history. A certain dialectic requires us to augment, or modify, or partially destroy the work of our predecessors in order to advance that art. Since it is a condition of the proper exercise of our art that we add to, refine, reconstruct and sometimes reject what we have inherited from earlier historians, the fact that we do so does not diminish our admiration of those historians, who in their time did to the work of others what we seek to do to their handiwork.

Ostensibly, the factors in modern history which Pollard deemed most important are revealed by the headings of the early chapters of his book: "Nationality," "The Advent of the Middle Class," "The New Monarchy," "Henry the Eighth and the Reformation," "Parliament," and "The Social Revolution," A close scrutiny of Pollard's argument, however, reveals that for him the roots of modernity are not quite so anarchically tangled as those chapter headings seem to indicate. In fact, there are but two interrelated, but not wholly interdependent, factors to consider — the emergence of the sovereign national state and the advent of the middle class. Having isolated these two factors in his first two chapters, in the remaining chapters Pollard describes their impact on the fabric of sixteenth- and seventeenth-century society.

Thus, the chapter on "The New Monarchy" demonstrates the triumphant political embodiment of the principle of nationality in the persons of the monarchs of the sixteenth century. The chapters on "Henry the Eighth and the Reformation" and on "Parliament" show how in that century the concurrent aims and aspirations of the national sovereign and of the middle class combined to break England's links with Rome and to enhance the importance of the House of Commons. And so on. The essence of the matter is that the middle class and the national state destroyed the dominance of the Catholic Church and feudalism, which were the twin pillars of the Middle Ages. Thus, by the operation of these two factors, medieval history ended and modern history began.

Fifty years after the publication of *Factors in Modern History*, few historians would deny that eventually in the Western World the middle-class men of the towns and of trade came to exercise a power in both the economic and the political sphere

that surpassed and supplanted that of the landed aristocracy. Few also would deny that in that world a passionate identification with the national state superseded an identification with the universal Church as the center of men's ultimate loyalties. The doubts that Pollard's arguments might encounter today would not be directed toward these two facts, but toward his chronology. Was the middle class quite so important, quite so masterful, *in the sixteenth century,* as Pollard thought it was? Was the national state quite so predominant in power, quite so pre-eminent among the loyalties of men, *in the sixteenth century,* as Pollard supposed? To both these questions the answer of most present-day historians probably would be "No."

On the first question, the question of the middle class, it is unnecessary to spend much time here. . . . It may be worth mentioning here, however, that some of the methods by which historians have tried to prove the dominance of men of the town and trade in sixteenth-century England and sixteenth-century Europe have been a trifle peculiar. For example, a gauge which measures the power of a class by the number of its members who bought their way out of it and on to the land, and by the speed with which they did so, is a very ambivalent instrument indeed; and the data that it renders call for great care in interpretation. Although a suspicion that the middle class was not rising in the sixteenth century in quite the way formerly alleged has taken hold among professional specialists, it has scarcely corrupted the sweet and innocent minds of the writers of textbooks, in whose works that class continues to ascend for six centuries or so in a smooth Pollardian way. But in matters of this sort a lag of three or four decades is to be expected among the writers of history textbooks, and we historians are nothing if not patient.

The myth of the national state will probably prove even more durable than the myth of the middle class.

As to the role Pollard ascribed to the

national state in the sixteenth century, a role to which he imputed pan-European import, one can but feel that here he was the victim of anachronism, induced by an insular myopia prevalent in his day. It is the myopia most notoriously advertised in the tiresome old story about the English newspaper headline, "Fog Over Channel. Continent Isolated." As a consequence of focusing his attention on England, and of generalizing for Europe from what he saw in England, Pollard ascribed to the political nation in the sixteenth century a dynamic force as fact and ideal that it had scarcely acquired in most of Europe until the nineteenth century. Even beyond that, he may well have exaggerated the national element in England itself. If we look at the British Isles from the continent rather than the other way about, we may be inclined to minimize, rather than maximize the role of nationality. Should we emphasize nationality, for example, as Pollard does, in accounting for the Protestant Reformation in England and Germany? In practical effect the religious conflict in Germany was settled in 1555 by leaving the determination of the religion of their own principalities in the hands of scores of sovereign princelings of the Holy Roman Empire. About this settlement there was nothing national. Noting that from 1530 to 1560 England passed from Roman Catholicism to English Catholicism to moderate Protestantism, to radical Protestantism, to Roman Catholicism, and back to moderate Protestantism again, a German observer might draw his own conclusions. Since each of these frequent shifts in the religion of England took place at the command of the current sovereign, our German friend might be pardoned for concluding that things in England were pretty much the way they were at home, that the will of the prince had a good deal to do with the religion of the region, and that nationality had precious little to do with it.

In general, it would seem that at various times and in various regions of Europe in the sixteenth century the sense of belonging to a nation was an element of varying intensity; that the people who in present-day jargon were in positions of decision-making took national sentiment into account and exploited it — as they took into account and exploited other kinds of sentiment — when such exploitation was feasible; but that such people were themselves rarely dominated by national feeling. On the role of national interest in the sixteenth century Professor Garrett Mattingly, whose vast but lightly-worn learning and unfailingly shrewd judgment have earned for his opinions a universal respect, says:

National interest was still too vague a concept to guide or even to excuse the policies of the monarchies. When the spokesman for the Estates General of 1506 besought Louis XII not to marry his daughter, the heiress of Brittany, to any but the natural heir to France, when an independent member of Parliament grumbled that the last English war across the Channel had cost more than twenty such ungracious dog-holes as its conquest, Thérouanne, would be worth . . . perhaps these citizens were fumbling toward what the nineteenth century would have regarded as a valid idea of the national interest. But their notions were still unformed. Mostly the third estates wanted just peace and lower taxes, and their infrequent murmurings were dismissed by their betters as the petty and short-sighted views of tradesmen unfit to meddle with the affairs of princes (*Renaissance Diplomacy*, p. 162).

In fairness to Pollard, one must add that Elizabeth and some of her advisors may have constituted an exception to Mattingly's rule.

Besides moderating his emphasis on nationalism and the middle class, historians writing fifty years after *Factors in Modern History* might want to stress some aspects of European history from the fifteenth to the seventeenth century that Pollard paid little attention to. Certainly they would say a great deal more about the Price Revolution, the gradual, but cumulatively spectacular, increase in the dearness of things that resulted from the augmentation of Europe's supply of precious metals in the sixteenth century. To the impact of the shift in price structure on the economy of the Western world, and on its social structure, Pollard devotes scarcely a paragraph, whereas that shift has become the framework on which many present-day historians hang their account of economy and society in Europe from about 1500 to 1650. It is not, however, quite sure that this has been all pure gain. There is a growing suspicion that when the historical dust has settled a bit, it will be discovered that the importance recently ascribed to the influx of gold and silver from America has been somewhat excessive.

With respect to another omission in *Factors in Modern History* there would be something close to unanimity among present-day historians. In a book devoted to the discovery of the roots of modernity in the sixteenth and seventeenth centuries they would look for the names of Copernicus, Kepler, Galileo, and Huygens, of William Gilbert, William Harvey, Robert Boyle and Isaac Newton — and in Pollard's book they would look in vain. Those names do not appear. This omission reveals a decisive change in the content of historical study during the past fifty years. The branch of that study called the history of ideas and the branch of that branch called the history of science have flourished mightily since 1907. This massive development of knowledge has left no doubt that the Scientific Revolution was a decisive turning point in the history of Western thought, possibly *the* decisive turning point in the history of the human mind. Historians today might feel, with Pollard, that to thrust the events of the sixteenth century into the medieval pigeonhole would burst the joints of that already overstuffed repository. Yet most of those historians would probably be reluctant to ascribe modernity to sixteenth-century men, whose world was still the closed hierarchical organic cosmos that medieval schoolmen had constructed by blending scripture, Aristotle, and Ptolemy, and not the infinite, mechanical universe that Kepler, Galileo, and Newton

built. And this is but to say that one matter, which seemed fairly settled in the 1900s, has since become quite unsettled — the matter of periods in history, of how best to divide into manageable segments the onward flow of events in time. Pollard was reasonably confident that it made sense to place the divide between medieval and modern history in the sixteenth century. Today doubts about the wisdom of selecting this particular line of division merge with yet graver doubts about the actuality, and even the convenience, of the very concepts, medieval and modern. It may be — and it will not be for the first time — that a loss of certainty stands at the beginning of knowledge.

In the past fifty years, historians have not only broadened our understanding of the sixteenth century; they have also refined it, made it more precise. To describe what has taken place in the refining of our historical analysis is not easy, since it has been a bit-by-bit process, whose general purport has not attracted much attention even from those engaged in it. So if my exposition seems a little shaky at this point, it is because it rests on home-made, and not well-made, foundations. In brief, it seems to me that the historical researches of the last five decades have revealed the sixteenth century to be an era during which the lines of class interest and national interest were traversed and frequently — perhaps more frequently than not — dominated by other lines of allegiance and action. We may best envisage these other lines as polar pairs, pulling men in opposite directions and therefore creating tensions. These tensions confronted sixteenth-century men with the multitude of particular decisions that they had to make.

Two of the polar pairs — Catholic–Protestant and Church–State — have long been in use by historians. Pollard deals with them. He more or less identifies Catholic with Church and Protestant with State. Then — in accord with his conception of the prime factors in modern history — he assimilates Catholic and Church to universal–feudal–medieval on the one hand, Protestant and State to national–middle-class–modern on the other. This propensity, strong in Pollard and his contemporaries and still strong today, seems to mark the triumph of a desire for simple order over a desire to face the facts. For in the sixteenth century Protestantism, especially in its Calvinist version, was *not* markedly middle-class. It attracted Norfolk and Gelderland squires and the Western Highlanders as powerfully as it did burghers in London, Amsterdam and Edinburgh. And it was the "internationalism" of the Calvinists — their readiness to render material aid and undergo bodily danger to render assistance to the persecuted Saints in foreign lands — that prevented the Papal counter-offensive from destroying Protestantism. The conviction which Calvinism ultimately developed with respect to the relation of State to Church received its most eloquent expression when the Scottish minister, Andrew Melville, plucked that would-be divine-right monarch James VI of Scotland by the sleeve, called him "God's silly vassal," and informed him that, although James was King of Scotland, Jesus Christ was King of the Kingdom of the Church, "whose subject King James VI is, and of whose Kingdom not a King . . . nor a head but a member." And Melville adds that the ministry "whom Christ has called and commanded to watch over His church have sufficient power . . . of Him so to do . . . the which no Christian prince should control or discharge." To the convinced Calvinist, the *Regnum Christi* was not a promise of pie in the sky but a call to present action. To many a European prince it was a clear and present danger. Until we grasp that the claims of Presbytery were *not* national or middle-class, that they were quite as universal, quite as catholic, and, in that dubious sense, quite as medieval, as the claims of the Papacy, we shall ill understand the events of the later sixteenth century. But then the taxonomy that completely subsumes Catholic under medieval and feudal is itself peculiar. It is a somewhat arbitrary way to classify a faith which flourished almost twenty centuries ago in the great cities of imperial Rome and which today enjoys firm support among the urban populace of the greatest cities of industrial America.

The study of sixteenth-century history during the past fifty years, then, has not sustained Pollard's decision to assimilate Protestantism and the defection from universalism to each other, and to reduce them to epiphenomena thrown up by the rise of the middle class and of nationalism. In Karl Marx's language, neither is mere superstructure. Moreover, during the past fifty years, historians of various aspects of the sixteenth century, as we have noted, have felt impelled to deal with other polarities besides Catholic–Protestant and Church–State. Among them are town–hinterland, lay–clerical, secular–religious, *Realpolitik*–legitimacy, realm–province, dynasty–region, *gubernaculum–jurisdictio,* court–country. No more than the Catholic–Protestant polarity will these others fit the patterning of history that makes the sixteenth century the great divide between feudal–universal–medieval on the one hand and middle-class–national–modern on the other. But although we recognize this one *negative* similarity, we must not conceive of these other polarities as complete historical analogues to the Catholic–Protestant polarity. For in the common opinion of the sixteenth century, the Catholic–Protestant polarity was absolute, unconditional. That is to say, both Catholic and Protestant claimed to possess the sole, saving, and God-given truth, necessary for the redemption of man. The logic of both the Catholic and the Protestant position, therefore, called for unremitting warfare on the opposite position. The principle was one of mutual exclusion, indeed of mutual extermination. If we adopt this point of view in examining the other polarities we have mentioned, however, we court confusion, for the Catholic–Protestant pair is eccentric, atypical in its absoluteness. Although between the opposed members of each of the other pairs there is tension, the issue is *never* either–or; it is *always* more-or-less. With respect to the interests of town and hinterland, of laity and clergy, of dynasty and region, of court and country, the question in the sixteenth century is never how one can annihilate the other; it is how to strike a viable balance between them, how under varying conditions to work out ever anew the terms of adjustment and reconciliation.

Failure to keep this point in mind can be fatal to our understanding of the sixteenth century, and nowhere more so than in grasping the relationship between *Realpolitik*, or political realism, and legitimacy. We are likely — as Pollard did — to note the discrepancy between the sixteenth-century statesman's profession of concern for the rightful public order of Christendom and his complete opportunism in practice, and to write off the profession as a cynical bit of fraudulence. By parity of reason we then ascribe the stateman's frequent advocacy of legality in the internal affairs of his master's realm to hypocrisy, too. Yet it is more likely that the major statesmen of the age — Gattinara and Perronet, Robertet and L'Hôpital, Cecil and Walsingham, even Wolsey and Thomas Cromwell — were *both* political realists *and* men concerned with legitimacy. The trouble was that, in the sphere of relations *among* rulers, the medieval structure of institutions was wholly shattered and afforded no foothold for aspirations toward a legitimate order. In this sphere men with power might talk, and even believe, the old pieties; but they acted, perforce, like a gang of disingenuous cannibals. Within the realm, however, where much of the framework of institutions remained relatively intact, the gap between profession and practice, between what men of power felt it right to do and what they felt it necessary and desirable to do, was a good bit smaller. In this sphere a concern for legitimacy had something substantial to hang on to. If this is so, then between the professions and the intentions of people like Henry VIII and Elizabeth I there may be a closer correspondence than most historians have been willing to grant.

Among the polarities mentioned earlier there are two that may be worth a little further discussion, because it seems likely that in the near future a good deal of the historical writing on the sixteenth century will focus on them, or at least it seems desirable that such writing should. They are dynasty–region and court–country. We have already watched Garrett Mattingly make short work of the illusion that national interest was the guiding star on which sixteenth-century monarchs set the course of their policy. But if not on national interest, on what did they set their course? Professor Mattingly says,

The sixteenth-century struggle for power had a *dynastic,* not a national, orientation. The Kingdom of Naples and the Duchy of Milan were wealthy and famous provinces. The conquest of either would increase the apparent strength of the prince who could effect it, and indubitably increase, for a time, the benefits he would be able to bestow on his captains and councilors. Whether such conquests would be worth to his people the blood and treasure they cost was an irrelevant, absurd question. Nobody expected that they would (*Renaissance Diplomacy,* pp. 152–3).

What counted most in high politics in Europe from 1450 to 1550 was not the French or English nation, much less the German or Italian nation. It was the Houses of Tudor, and Valois, and Burgundy, and Trastamara, and Hapsburg; and when dynasticism attained its fullest development and its greatest eccentricity, it was the monster House of Trastamara-Burgundy-Hapsburg, embodied in the person of Charles V.

At the pole opposite to the dynasty was not the nation; that much is certain. But to give a name to what was at the opposite pole is not easy. The word "region" may be the best word available; but it is most unsatisfactory. It is as near as one can come in English to the more satisfactory but not perfect French word, *pays*. In the sense intended here France, England, and possibly Spain were *pays,* but hardly Germany or Italy. And, although they were parts of the *pays de France,* Brittany, Languedoc, and Burgundy were also *pays.* Aragon was a *pays,* and so were the parts of Aragon called Catalonia and Valencia. In the first half of the sixteenth century the Netherlands were one *pays* comprised of about a dozen *pays.* Ireland was a *pays,* and so was Wales, and so, possibly, was the region that Englishmen simply called the North; but Sussex and Wiltshire were not. What then, constituted a *pays,* or, understood simply as a translation of that word, a region? Roughly, a *pays* or region was a territory whose inhabitants shared a sentiment of identification with that territory and with each other, sufficiently strong to make it regularly necessary for politicians to take that sentiment into account in their political decisions. The more resistant regions almost always had regional liberties, charters, *fueros,* well-preserved ancient customs. They often had special regional political organs, too, which enabled them to do some highly effective foot-dragging when dynastic policy ran overmuch against the regional interest. It was not the nation that set limits to the pursuit of dynastic policy in the sixteenth century; it was the *pays* or region. What the results might be, if the tension between dynasty and region ran too high, Philip II learned at great expense in his dealings with the Netherlands.

The court–country polarity is more difficult to define than the dynasty-region polarity, because in historical fact the boundary between court and country is far less distinct than the one between dynasty and region. Indeed, the effective monarch in the sixteenth century was precisely the one who prevented a sharp delimitation of those boundaries from taking place, who avoided the dangers inherent in the isolation of court from country. In England, for example, the grooms of the chamber and gentlemen-in-waiting were wholly court, the great officers of state only slightly less so. Lord-Lieutenants, on the other hand, were betwixt and between, half-court half-country; and the justices of the peace were almost wholly country. Roughly speaking, the court was at once a source of patronage, a focus of power, a way of life, and a repository of administrative authority at the center of which stood, not the abstract crown, but the living, breathing prince. Country was the miscellaneous lot of interests, concerns, and habits of thought and action that were essentially *local* in character, although certain local interests and concerns might be common to almost all the localities in a realm. Research into the internal development of European states that, explicitly or otherwise, takes fully into account the court–country polarity has not been under way for more than a decade or so. Implicitly it is taken into account in Sir John Neale's great work on the Elizabethan Parliaments and in the later sections of William Dunham's recent study of the fee'd retainer, explicitly in Trevor-Roper's *The Gentry.* A further orientation of research to the court–country polarity might at once add flesh to the lean history of sixteenth-century governance and provide some bones for the invertebrate mass called local history.

So far in this rather long-winded examination of an old book, we have dealt with matters of substance or body and matters of form or mind. In the Christian tradition, we ought to end up by dealing with the spirit; but pronouncements about the spirit of one's own day, or even of an earlier day, with respect to almost anything are tricky affairs. In this area, above all, each man is likely to confuse the voice of the age with the echo of his own prejudices and prepossessions. Nevertheless, the voice of the age — of any age — does speak from many mouths. The voice of Pollard's age certainly spoke from his. Notions, so much in the air at a particular time that the people of that time scarcely are aware of them, yet leave subtle but indelible marks on the things those people write. The assumptions historians make permeate their work by conditioning the way they order their data and the importance they ascribe to the various arrays of events that come under their consideration. At the moment we are not concerned with "inexplicit assumptions," dear to the hearts of practitioners of the sociology of knowledge. For Pollard makes at least one assumption with all the explicitness the heart could desire. He does so in such statements as: "There have been changes sudden in their outward manifestations. The French Revolution is a more striking example of them than the transition from medieval to modern history. But even the French Revolution was a summation of causes which had been working for ages. Even here it is true to say that *Natura nihil facit per saltum.*" Nature does nothing by leaps (*Factors in Modern History*, p. 33). Or again:

Whatever factors we take in the making of that change from medieval to modern history . . . they have their roots stretching far back into the past and buried far out of sight. The growth and decay are silent, gradual, almost imperceptible. The dramatic events which catch the eye and ear, and by which we date the progress or backslidings of mankind, are, like the catastrophes which convulse the sphere of nature, but the outward and visible manifestations of causes, working without rest, without haste, without conscious human direction, in the making of the history of the world (*ibid.* p. 51).

Pollard's Latin tag — *Natura nihil facit per saltum* — is a dead giveaway. It dates *Factors in Modern History* very tidily as the intellectual emanation of a period when the idea of progress and, indeed, the whole domain of social thought in general had taken on the color and tone of Darwinism. It comes earlier than the emergence of those doubts about the gradualness of transformations in the sphere of organic nature, which were engendered by the study of genetics. If I have not got mutation theory all mixed up — and I probably have — biologists today would be likely to suggest that organic nature does nothing important in the way of change *except* by jumps. But for historians of an era precommitted to

find in human history an analogue to the process of gradual, even glacial, change that they believed characteristic of natural history, the particular sort of factor analysis which Pollard adopted was something of a godsend. Consider Pollard's own procedure. As we have seen, he selects as the crucial factors in modern history the advent of the middle class and nationalism. Now the middle class and nationalism did not exist in Europe in the tenth century. They may perhaps be dimly discernible in the twelfth century; they attain undeniable ascendancy only in the nineteenth century. Since we start with the middle class and nationalism at low ebb, and, about six hundred years later, end up with them at high flood, what more natural for a historian committed to evolutionary gradualism than to connect the starting point and the end point on his time scale in the simplest way possible — by an ascending straight line. Pollard and his contemporaries did the natural thing: they drew that straight line. And ever since in the pages of our history textbooks, "emerging nationalism" and the "rising middle class" century after century have toiled steadily upward along it.

In fact, there is no reason to assume that the slopes of the curves of ascent of the middle class and of nationalism during more than half a millennium were straight lines, or even that they trended continuously upward over their whole course. To work out empirical methods just for roughly gauging the slope of such a curve over its whole course would tax the ingenuity of the shrewdest analytical historian. Naturally Pollard was not aware that his views involved any empirical problem of measurement. That straight line of his is wholly *a priori*, a purely imaginary construction that does not set historical facts in order, but altogether escapes and soars above their dreary restrictions. It is the product not of historical investigations but of the spirit of Pollard's age, the age of historical Darwinism.

If we give serious consideration to those varied polarities mentioned above, our very image of the historical process will differ drastically from Pollard's. The sense of inevitable, straight-line trends, so strong in him, diminishes. The sense of the catastrophic, which Pollard minimizes, increases. For a while at the turn of the fifteenth century, the tensions among various poles stand in rough and complex balance, and the adjustments necessary to maintain a workable equilibrium are relatively small. Then a couple of wholly unpredictable things happen. Luther successfully defies the Pope; the conquistadors discover the precious metal hoards and mines of America. Within a few decades these events drastically augment the tensions in the system. The areas in which men can get along on the more-or-less type of decision shrink. The areas in which they have to face either–or decisions expand. As such decisions increase in number, they also increase in importance; both what decisions will have to be made next, and what their proximate consequences will be, become increasingly hard for contemporaries to predict, and the stream of happenings flows not with glacial majesty but with devastating violence.

The catastrophic character of history at times of crises is reflected in the kind of history writing that can deal with such times. Analytical history, the sort of history that Pollard wrote in *Factors,* and the sort that has become increasingly popular in academic circles since, runs into trouble amid the convulsions of a world in upheaval. It often pretends that they really weren't convulsions, or that they really didn't matter. But, of course, they really were convulsions, and they really did matter. At this point, the narrative historian must take over from the analytical historian; for it is his art not to demonstrate that the course of events was inevitable, but, in the midst of mounting uncertainties, to render the decisions men made intelligible.

And here, in the past fifty years, our movement has not been progressively forward, or even, crablike, sideways; but

simply backward. Living in the tradition of both Macaulay and Ranke, A. F. Pollard did not need to be told that history is an intricate sequence of the acts of men in time; and that ultimately, to do justice to that sequence, one needs to tell a story. That his own volume in the Political History of England series, written in 1910, remains even now the best single treatment of the era it covers sufficiently testifies to Pollard's mastery of narrative. Today, however, orthodox academic historians tend to put story-telling under a ban. To tell a story well is to commit the scandalous sin of being popular if one is not an academic, or of being a romantic historian if one is an academic. Putting story-telling under a ban does not, of course, make it possible to traverse the period between say, Luther's breach with Rome and the Edict of Nantes without telling a story. It does, however, make it possible for some academic historian to tell such stories incompetently while smugly regarding their ineptitude as an infallible mark of redemptive merit, of their superiority to those damned historians who tell their stories well.

Having dealt with an explicit assumption that colored Pollard's view of what happened in modern history, we may conclude this essay with a brief examination of one of his tacit or inexplicit assumptions. This assumption is still current among many historians, and in all likelihood it remains tacit, I suspect, because historians are not aware that they are making it. Since the assumption is not directly expressed, it is rather difficult to find the right words to describe it. The assumption of the conservation of historical energy is reasonably satisfactory, although the wages-fund theory of the historical process, or the teeter totter or seesaw theory, might do just as well. The model in this instance, one may guess, was taken from Newtonian physics rather than from Darwinian natural history. Stated rather abstractly, the idea is that in a given society the energy expended on a single pair of polar elements is fixed, so that any flow of social energy in the direction of one such pole can only take place by way of subtraction from the flow of energy to the opposite pole. So abstractly stated, the idea, I fear, may seem trivial, or unintelligible, or both. Let us try to make it a little more concrete. Earlier we mentioned secular and regious as polar phenomena. In so doing, we aimed to point up the contrast between aspirations and actions directed toward this-worldly and those directed toward other-worldly goals. Granted that in particular cases it is not always possible to make a clear-cut distinction, still, to suggest an extreme instance, it is not too hard to decide toward which pole the lustful glutton tends, and toward which the martyr, toward which Alexander VI and toward which Savonarola. Now, on the assumption of the conservation of historical energy, if in a society there is an increase of activity in the direction of the secular pole, there *must* be a corresponding decrease of energy in the direction of the religious pole. Moreover and therefore, for the historian who makes the assumption, *the increase in the secular direction is itself sufficient evidence of the decrease in the religious direction.* Although this corollary to the assumption of the conservation of historical energy is an intellectual trap of the most lethal sort, I fear that the abstractness of my exposition still conceals the clear, present, and practical danger which I have been trying to reveal. Perhaps the surest, if not the kindest, way to reveal the danger of this trap is to show what happens when someone falls into it.

In *Factors in Modern History,* A. F. Pollard falls into it. Throughout his book, but especially in the chapter on "Henry the Eighth and the Reformation," Pollard makes a very good case for the intensification of this-worldliness in the sixteenth century. And he does not nearly exhaust the evidence supporting his case. Consider the boast of Elizabethan statesmen — a strangely secular boast in view of the Christian tradition in such matters — that they intended to punish no one for his religious beliefs. Consider the French *politiques* — French Catholics, who yet preferred the hope of this-worldly peace, held out by the Edict of Nantes, to their Christian duty to extirpate heresy. Consider even Philip of Spain, who, long after the Pope had excommunicated the English Jezebel, was still ready to negotiate for a peaceful settlement of his differences with her.

The evidence, then, strongly indicates that many sixteenth-century men aimed at, and even openly avowed, secular goals which almost all men of the thirteenth century would have rejected with an outward show of horror and, quite possibly, with real inward loathing. These being the facts about this-worldliness, the secular, in the sixteenth century, what inferences about other-worldliness, about the religious, can we properly draw from them? The answer, of course, is that we can properly draw no inferences whatever about other-worldliness in the sixteenth century from these facts. Any commitment with respect to other-worldliness in the sixteenth century, that is, with respect to any historical phenomenon in any century, should follow and never precede the historical investigation of that phenomenon at that time. It must not be derived from the investigation of the opposite or polar phenomenon alone. Yet without a moment of hesitation Pollard, and a great many historians since Pollard, have habitually, perhaps even unconsciously, inferred from the facts about this-worldliness in the sixteenth century the decline of other-worldliness in that age. Why did Pollard do it? He did it because he had fallen into the lethal trap I have been trying not very successfully to describe, the trap created by the corollary about evidence which follows from his assumption about the conservation of historical energy. He took the demonstrable increase in the flow of energy and activity to the secular pole to be adequate evidence of the flow of activity and energy away from the religious pole. And here in a quite concrete instance the assumption about the conservation of historical energy has exercised a practical and very malign influence on historical imagination. Since they have already *taken it as given* that other-worldliness declined in the sixteenth century, Pollard and many other historians have had either to disregard facts which suggest that things were otherwise or they have had to explain such facts away. Neither alternative is a very happy one, since both, instead of helping us to make sense of one of the most conspicuous sequences of facts in the sixteenth century, force us to make nonsense of it. That conspicuous sequence of facts is the one which runs from the religious revival, exemplified but not exhausted by Christian humanism, through the Reformation and the Counter-Reformation, to the Wars of Religion. That this series of events indicates that the sixteenth century underwent an intensity and extension of religious concern beyond anything which had been experienced or imagined in the fifteenth century is a historical inference practically beyond doubt.

Only something *extra-historical* could blind able historians to a fact so obvious. We have identified that extra-historical entity — the assumption of the conservation of historical energy. If we get rid of the assumption, we get rid of our difficulty and can look squarely at the historical facts. Once we realize that the religious and the secular, although polar to one another, *can,* both at once, rise to higher levels of intensity, we will recognize that they both *did* so rise in the sixteenth century. From 1517 on, the religious revival which had begun earlier got caught up in the one historical polarity of the sixteenth century which was unconditional and absolute — the polarity between Catholic and Protestant. Under such circumstances its very intensity threatened the civil order and the security of every land in Western Christendom. But men — almost all men — are concerned not only with matters of creed and ideology; they are also concerned with civil order, which is the framework of their living from day to day. And for secular rulers the maintenance of civil order is at once a necessity and, according to the views current in the sixteenth century, a part of their duty to God. When the intensified pull toward the religious pole found expression in mortal strife between Catholic and Protestant, is it really any wonder that men of theory, like Bodin, felt impelled to think through afresh the problem of political obligation, that men of judgment, like Montaigne, felt the need to dampen the fires of sectarian ardor, and that statesmen, regardless of their religious preference, felt driven to play the European power game with a cold and careful calculation of the consequences of each move? Whether in the particular situation domestic order, or place in the European state system, or both, were involved, the conflict over religion had set a painfully high price on errors or weakness in the game of power in the sixteenth century. So Mary Stuart learned to her cost in Scotland, and Philip II to his cost in the Netherlands. So the French learned through a generation of devastating and bloody religious civil war. If, in the sixteenth century, many men displayed an intense preoccupation with chilly computations of this-worldly advantage, it was in part at least because they felt at their backs the burning heat of religious conflagration.

It was my intention to bring this essay to a close with an apology for its scantiness in the *matter* of history, the massing of fact, and for its preoccupation with the *forms* of historical explanation. Yet after all, had the deployment of a mass of fact seemed more desirable to me on this occasion than a contemplation of problems of historical form, there was nothing to prevent such a deployment. But history writing is more than a piling up of facts; it is an arraying, an ordering of facts. Its goal is not only to state what happened, but to render what happened increasingly intelligible; and we must concern ourselves not only with ways of getting data, but with ways of putting data together. Our refined methods of assessing evidence and establishing facts, of which we are justly proud, should not be the only tools of our craft. Historians need to be a most eclectic band of workers, jacks-of-many-trades, if not of all. We should be ready to bring to bear on the problems of ordering intelligibly those facts at our disposal, the whole range of our remembered experiences — what we know about other disciplines, the insights we have gained from literature, and, perhaps most important, though surely least cultivated, a certain good sense and solidity of judgment which we may acquire if we go reflectively about the business of living our own lives. In the indispensable fervor of collecting vast stacks of 4 in. by 6 in. cards, covered with priceless, although somewhat incoherent bits of information, let us not forget what Pollard knew so well and exemplified so clearly in *Factors in Modern History*: "He also serves," who sometimes sits and thinks.

SUGGESTIONS FOR ADDITIONAL READING

A comprehensive discussion of the recent literature on the subject we have dealt with is not available. The nearest thing to such a discussion is the article by Roland Mousnier and Fritz Hartung, "Quelques problèmes concernant la monarchie absolue," *Relazioni del X congresso internazionale di scienze storiche* (Florence, 1955), IV, *Storia Moderna*. Good discussions of the nature of sixteenth century political institutions and the social and economic changes of the period can be found in any of the standard multi-volume histories now available. In the English series *The New Cambridge Modern History* there is the volume edited by G. R. Potter, *The Renaissance, 1493–1520* (Cambridge, 1957), and that edited by G. R. Elton, *The Reformation, 1520–1559* (Cambridge, 1958). The excellent French series *Peuples et Civilisations* contains *La fin du Moyen Âge* (Paris, 1931), part 2, *L'annonce des temps nouveaux*, edited by Henri Pirenne and others. In the same series there is the excellent volume to which Henri Hauser contributed heavily: *Les débuts de l'âge moderne* (Paris, 1956). Roland Mousnier's *Les XVIe et XVIIe siecles* (Paris, 1961), vol. IV of *Histoire générale des civilisations*, is an excellent recent synthesis. The great German scholar Gerhard Ritter is the general editor of the series *Geschichte der Neuzeit,* in which Erich Hassinger's *Das Werden des Neuzeitliche Europa* appeared in 1959. The leading multi-volume history by American scholars is *The Rise of Modern Europe,* in which two excellent volumes relevant to our theme, both containing important bibliographic essays, have appeared to date. These are Myron P. Gilmore's *The World of Humanism* (New York, 1952) and Carl Friedrich's *The Age of the Baroque* (New York, 1952).

More specialized studies in English are not nearly so easy to find. The literature dealing with the "New Monarchies," their antecedents and environment, is largely a European literature. But excellent studies of an advanced sort do exist. The economic institutions and social structure of the age of nascent absolutism and constitutional conflict is discussed in F. L. Nussbaum, *A History of the Economic Institutions of Modern Europe* (New York, 1933), a volume that summarizes the massive studies of Werner Sombart, whose *Der Bourgeois* remains a classic on the appearance of the middle class, despite its 1913 publication date. Important for the same background questions is the work of J. H. Hexter, *Reappraisals in History* (Evanston, 1961).

Specifically political institutions, especially parliamentary or representative institutions, their origins and early modern development in conflict with the centralizing tendencies of the Renaissance princes, are discussed in a number of important works. Pride of place must perhaps be allowed to Otto Hintze's "Weltgeschichtliche Bedingungen der Repräesentativeverfassung," which appeared in *Historische Zeitschrift,* CXLIII (1931), 1–47, where older ideas about the medieval origins of representative institutions are codified. Some of the same issues are discussed by F. Chabod, "Y a-t-il un état de la Renaissance," *Actes du colloque sur la Renaissance* (Paris, 1958), pp. 57–78, as well as in Hexter's volume mentioned above and Sir G. N. Clark's incisive *The Seventeenth Century* (Oxford, 1947). The 2nd part of a volume of essays presented to Helen Maud Cam, *Album Helen Maud Cam: Studies Presented to the International Commission for the History of Representative and Parliamentary Institutions,* XXIV (Louvain, 1961), contains several important essays on the subject here discussed. See especially the articles by B. Lyon, "Medieval Constitutionalism," 155–183, and F. L. Carsten, "The Causes of the Decline of the German Estates," 287–296. For England parliamentary institutions have a special significance, and English scholars and their American counterparts have contributed to our understanding of their role in the sixteenth century. The most important modern works are those by Sir John E. Neale, especially his *The Elizabethan House of Commons* (London, 1949) and his two-volume study of Queen Elizabeth's parliaments, entitled *Elizabeth I and her Parliaments* (London, 1953). Earlier studies by Wallace Notestein, *The Winning of the Initiative by the House of Commons* (London, 1926) and A. F. Pollard's *The Evolution of Parliament* (New York, 1926), are valuable for the light they throw on the use made of parliaments by the earlier Tudors. *Past and Present,* Number 25 (July, 1963), 3–59, contains a symposium on the Tudor State, focusing on Dr. Elton's "revolution," but with attention given to the views of Pollard and Professor Richardson, especially in the article by Dr. Penry Williams. For France the best recent works are those by J. Russell Major, whose monographs on various aspects of the Renaissance monarchy in France have contributed greatly to the revisionist school. In addition to the work reprinted here his *The Estates-General of 1560* (Princeton, 1951) and *The Deputies to the Estates General of Renaissance France* (Wisconsin, 1960), are especially important, the more so because he disagrees pointedly with Chabod and also with the leading Spanish authority, Jaime Vincen Vives. Two of Major's articles may also be mentioned: "The Loss of Royal Initiative and the Decay of the Estates-General in France, 1421–1615," *Album Helen Maud Cam: Studies Pre-* sented to the International Commission for the History of Representative and Parliamentary Institutions (Louvain, 1961), XXIV, 247–259; and "The French Renaissance Monarchy as seen through the Estates General," *Studies in the Renaissance,* IX (1962), 113–125. The available literature on the Netherlands is more slight, but Pieter Geyl, *The Revolt of the Netherlands* (London, 1958) and H. G. Koenigsberger's "The Organization of Revolutionary Parties in France and the Netherlands during the 16th Century," *Journal of Modern History,* XXVII (1955), 335–351, are useful.

There is not a very extensive literature on the development of royal or parliamentary administrative organs. The best treatment of bureaucracy and its role in the sixteenth century contest for power is found in the concluding chapters of G. E. Aylmer's *The King's Servants* (London, 1961), a work concerned with the civil service under Charles I, but which deals with the historical problem of political institutions and bureaucracy in England and on the Continent in a masterly fashion. For a comparative study of administrative developments and the role of office in royal government K. W. Swart's *The Sale of Office in the 17th Century* (The Hague, 1949), despite its title, is valuable for the earlier period. Finally, it needs to be said that the student wishing further insight into this aspect of the problem or, indeed, any other line of investigation, ought to go to the standard bibliographies and to the journals. All of the leading periodicals carry useful summaries of recent literature, as well as reviews of important works.